KU-154-327

The Multichannel Retail Handbook

A guide to planning, implementation, operation and enhancement

By Chris Jones

Copyright © Chris Jones 2013

All rights reserved

The right of Chris Jones to be identified as the Author of the Work has been asserted by him in accordance with the Copyright, Designs and Patents Act 1988.

ISBN 978-1-300-65266-3

First published in January 2013
by Redsock Management Ltd

Contents

Table of Figures

Introduction

Chapter 1.   Why multichannel?

1.1 It's where the money is

Many years ago, I went to a presentation given by the senior executive responsible for group strategy at a top global retailer. I was expecting rather sophisticated material, full of complex strategic concepts, probably somewhat over my head. Instead he described their strategy very simply with a famous quote: "follow the money"[1]. And that exactly sums up why multichannel is important to retailers today. If you currently operate already in a country like the UK, US or in Scandinavia, then you probably don't need persuading. But just to illustrate the point, **Figure 1** is a chart of brick-and-mortar (offline) versus online retail sales (adjusted for inflation) in the UK over the last 10 years.

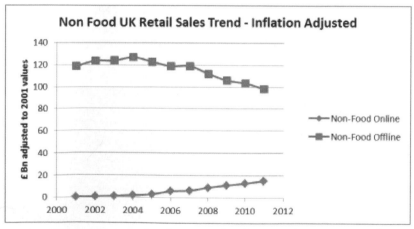

Figure 1 - non-food UK retail sales trend CPI adjusted[2]

There are lots of complex factors buried in the data, not least the credit crunch and the general reduction in prices caused by the growth

---

[1] In fact this is one of those historical quotes-that-never-was; it actually comes from the movie All The President's Men
[2] Source data: UK Office of National Statistics. CPI has been used as the inflation index measure

of imports from China. But the overall picture is starkly clear – there a huge ongoing shift in consumer spending away from brick-and-mortar stores to online channels. In the UK this extends as far as retailers now planning to downsize their stores estate in favour of investment in multichannel (see **Chapter 13**). The UK is an exceptional case, and in most countries this strategic switch is not yet appropriate. But I am aware of no (business-as-usual) country in the world where the share of online as a percentage of overall retail is declining. In most countries it is increasing rapidly.

Online penetration varies significantly category-by-category – some categories are much easier to translate to online than others. An example where online penetration is already extremely high is office products in the USA. **Figure 2** illustrates of the relative importance of non-store sales to the two market leading players, Staples and Office Depot.

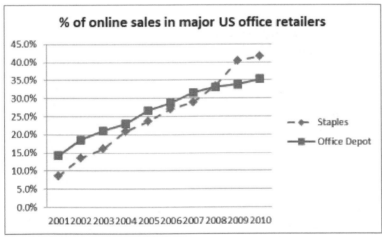

Figure 2 - Non-store as a % of total sales, US Office retailers 2001-2010[3]

In the case of Staples, over 40% of all sales are now non-store sales. When this percentage of your total sales comes from non-store, you'd better take following the money seriously. In fact, very seriously,

[3] As published by Staples and Office Depot in various places including annual company reports

because without non-store, total sales for Staples would actually have declined in the recession (*Figure 3*).

Figure 3 - Staples total sales, online vs brick-and-mortar[4]

This is not just a single retailer effect. The behaviour is replicated in almost all economies reasonably impacted by the credit crunch – growth in eCommerce has remained resilient despite the overall downturn.

1.2 It's where the growth is

If you are not following the money, you can be expecting to fight ongoing for a declining share of your customers' wallets. How quickly this happens will vary from country to country. Here's a look at the current trends in various geographies (*Figure 4*). Growth figures for countries like the US or UK may appear low, but they are starting from a much higher base in 2007; the average UK citizen spent more than 1700 USD online overall (i.e. not just retail) in 2011. Growth in *online* consumer spending in all countries far exceeds growth in *overall* consumer spending; globally and locally, the customer wallet is rapidly becoming an online wallet.

---

[4] ibid

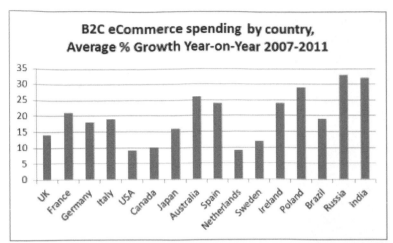

Figure 4 - country by country growth in B2C eCommerce[5]

The trend is even more marked at category level. In most countries, online B2C begins in travel – especially airline and rail tickets - and then the first true retail categories to see a significant shift into online are consumer electronics and media/books, which are (apparently) easier categories to implement, especially for online retail start-ups. For example in the Ukraine it is estimated that over 10% of all retail sales in consumer electronics are already online, and this is in a country where a general assessment of its eCommerce-readiness would place it pretty low down the charts.

I omitted China from Figure 4 because its year-on-year growth would have distorted the chart! We can compare overall Chinese retail growth on a quarter by quarter basis with the growth of B2C eCommerce (a very large percentage of eCommerce in China is currently C2C marketplace commerce, so it's necessary to exclude this from the data). *Figure 5* shows the growth curves as an index from a baseline in 2010. Yes, retail overall has grown slightly faster than Chinese GDP, reflecting the steady consumerisation of China, but much of this growth has come from online.

---

[5] Source: Ofcom International Market Communications Report 2012

Figure 5 – growth index for B2C online retail in China[6]

Half a billion (500,000,000) internet users can't be wrong...

If you are an online pure-play, all this growth represents an obvious opportunity to grab your slice of the pie. If you are a brick-and-mortar retailer, why would you want to give your market share away to these upstart online pure-plays? Much better to be there already!

1.3 It's where your customers are

You may well be thinking that the above data is all very nice, but it's about online eCommerce, not really multichannel retailing – the true blending of bricks and mortar with non-store. And this is where it gets really interesting. The headline is quite simple: the more channels you offer your customers to shop your retailers, the more they spend; or the other way around – multichannel customer spend more, known as the multichannel halo effect.

How much more is the subject of much debate, but data points anywhere from about 60% to 400%(!) have been quoted by major retailers who have attempted to measure the effect. Individual studies inevitably have different figures, but all show the same trend; an averaged out view of some typical studies produces a picture like *Figure 6*.

---

[6] Source: Chinese National Bureau of Statistics

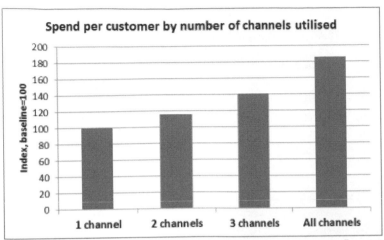

Figure 6 – Multichannel customers spend more[7]

It's important to note that not all of these channels are necessarily transactional channels. Customers don't need to be able to make a purchase on four or more channels for you to see this effect. They do, however, need to be able to meet you on four or more channels. *Figure 7* shows a typical purchase journey:

---

[7] See for example studies by IDC 2009, Accenture 2009, ORC 2010, Deloitte 2010

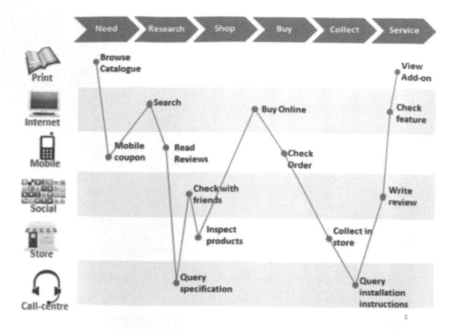

Figure 7 - an omni-channel purchase

The rise of the Omni-Channel Shopper is a step change in customer behaviour, driven by the growth of multichannel retail. Not only do consumers expect you to be on all the channels they are using, but if you are not – if there's a "break in the chain" – then they'll quickly shift to a competitor: in fact around 50%[8] of them will immediately look to a competitor if you don't offer them a transition between channels... at each step of their purchase journey.

Multichannel is where your customers are. If you're there too, they'll spend more. If you're not, they'll more than likely go spend with a competitor. And in fact, your best customers are most likely to be the ones who will expect to be able access you via more than one channel. So your best customers are also the ones most likely to depart to a competitor if you don't meet their multichannel needs!

Losing customers to your competitors is not good, and so it is becoming more and more essential to ensure their multichannel

---

[8] See for example various studies by Accenture 2008 or Deloitte 2010

needs are indeed met. The objective of this book is to try and help you do so.

1.4 Top Takeaways

There is a major shift in spending underway from brick-and-mortar to online channels.

In some retailers online sales now represent over 40% of all sales.

Online sales have proven generally recession-proof during recent years.

Growth in consumer spending *online* has far exceeded *general* growth in all countries.

Multichannel customers spend up to 400% more than other customers.

Your best customers are more likely to demand a multichannel experience. Half of them may exit to a competitor if you don't offer an option when they attempt to switch channels mid-purchase.

The rise of the omni-channel customer is a step-change in customer behaviour, driven by multichannel.

Chapter 2.   About this book

2.1 Structure overview

This book is divided into four parts.

Part A – Proposition – examines the processes involved in defining a multichannel proposition for your customers that is appropriately differentiated from your competitors.

Part B – Fundamentals – considers a number of key building blocks which are common to all propositions involving online retail in some way, be it simply adding a new online channel to existing brick-and-mortar retail, or more complex "true" multichannel.

Part C – Basics – is essentially a guide for a currently brick-and-mortar retailer who wants to add an online channel. It could also be a guide to creating an online pure-play eCommerce retailer, but my scope intentionally excludes those aspects of retail which are not significantly different online from offline; for example there is no "how to manage a supply chain" chapter, but there is included a discussion of how the logistics of direct-to-customer fulfilment varies from the logistics of brick-and-mortar store replenishment. It is structured around building the cost-benefit case.

Part D – From Multiple Channel to Multichannel – looks at taking the big step between having brick-and-mortar stores plus an eCommerce channel through to linking all channels together in a truly multichannel way.

The book is intended to be read sequentially, so that each part, and in fact each chapter, builds on material from the previous ones. Nevertheless I have tried where possible to ensure that each chapter can also be read standalone; I recognise that my target audience may want to read only those sections relevant to their current priorities. I have also briefly summarised the key points of each chapter in its concluding section entitled Top Takeaways.

2.2 A note on data points

One of the most vexing issues in studying multichannel retail is the absence of well-founded, publicly available, quantitative data points. There is a huge amount of data. No self-respecting software or solutions vendor is without a white paper or two, demonstrating how vital their product is to your sales curve, supported by suitable data. Retailers themselves do occasionally publish useful data or facts about their own operations or customers, but these tend to be those that present the retailer in a flattering light to its stakeholders. Other data, even if positive, is often commercially sensitive and therefore unpublished for obvious reasons. Where I have worked myself with retailers and am therefore aware of specific data, I am bound by client-confidentiality.

Quoting genuinely independent data points in support of some of the assertions in this book is thus unusually challenging. I have therefore adopted one the following approaches:

i) Where, based on my own broad experience, I believe a data point to be generally valid, I have either cited a specific representative example with an endnote reference (usually supported by an endnote starting "see for example...") or else simply stated the data point and suggested places the interested reader might look further

ii) Where I believe a data point to be worth quoting because it feels to me valid based on experience but lacks support from other similar studies, I have stated this explicitly

iii) In a few cases I have wanted to illustrate a lack of consensus or general confusion around a topic. In these cases I have noted explicitly that the data points have been plucked somewhat at random from reasonably credible, but nevertheless conflicting or possibly self-serving, sources

iv) Where I have assembled public-domain data into a chart or graph to illustrate the point I am trying to make, I have stated the public-domain source of this data in the endnotes (typically a government statistics or trade federation websites). Be warned that even official government statistics are often in conflict.

Multichannel retail is a very fast moving field. This book was written in the fourth quarter of 2012. I have quoted recent examples or statistics where these are available.

Frequently data points are associated with monetary values in some way. I have tried where possible to use global examples, which are therefore in varying currencies. At the time of writing, exchange rates were approximately as follows (*Figure 8*):

1	GBP	British Pounds
= 1.25	EUR	Euros
= 1.55	AUD	Australian Dollars
=1.60	USD	US Dollars

Figure 8 - Exchange Rates

Many of the non-governmental data-sources used may have a commercial interest in publishing their chosen statistics. Throughout this book I am implying no endorsement or otherwise of any sources mentioned, nor on the rare occasions where I have named products or solutions are these meant to imply a recommendation or otherwise; all such examples are for illustration only.

2.3 Feedback

Constructive feedback is always welcome, and I will endeavour to reply (once) to any received. You can contact me at this email address: handbook@redsock.biz

2.4 Style

I am a practising freelance consultant, my clients expect advice as well as just information, and advice is inevitably – especially in such a young discipline – partly subjective. It seemed to me that a less formal "I talk to you" style is therefore inherently more honest for this book. I can at least promise that any recommendations or suggestions made herein are unbiased by any considerations other than my own preferences and experiences.

Therefore: I hope you find this book useful.

Part A – Proposition

Chapter 3.   Where to start?

3.1 Moscow, 1960

Moscow, March 1960, seems like a good place to start.

Figure 9 - Moscow 1960[9]

This is one of the best-known positions in the history of chess, taken from a famous world championship game. Why is a chess position relevant to multichannel retailing? Well, a strong chess player, reasonably educated in the chess-classics, will be able to recognise this position reliably after seeing it for less than a single second.[10] Not even a grandmaster, just a reasonably strong player, can digest and assess the information presented on all 64 squares on a chess board in around 0.8 seconds. Most of us, of course, are not expert chess players, but from constant practice we are expert

---

[9] Tal-Botvinnik, World Championship Match Moscow 1960, Game 6: 21. ... Nf4?!

[10] See for example Hartston & Wason, The Psychology of Chess, 1983

shoppers. And once we get used to them, we are also expert users of our internet browsers, mobile phones, tablets. Just like the expert chess player rapidly assessing a position, our expertise as shoppers and as device-users means we can assess the content of a complex retail screen full of information in less than a second.

Take a look again at the example shopping journey presented in **Figure 7**. There are *at least* 9 basic screen-based interactions involved in this purchase, and countless actual screens. And on every single screen, the customer has a vital decision to take (Figure 10).

Figure 10 - Decisions decisions

And it takes them *one second* to make that decision. Because this is so important, it's worth giving a name to, for use later in this book: so henceforth, this is the One Second Rule. It is perhaps the simplest illustration of two of the biggest paradigm shifts that most traditional brick-and-mortar retailers have to come to terms with when tackling multichannel:

- The customer has much more power

- Everything happens faster; not just customer interaction, but the retailer operating cycle too

Take the simple example of a customer browsing your shop. If you've got them through the door of a brick-and-mortar store, you have all sorts of advantages: your staff can approach the customer and try to sell them something; the customer can't leave without walking through the store – which might take as long as a few minutes in a hypermarket; you can place tempting merchandise just in the customer's eye-line, like all those treats and magazines next to the checkout. By contrast, if you get a customer browsing your store online, you can't approach them, their eye-line might well be another application (possibly a competitor's) open on the same device or another device, and if they want to leave you it's just a matter of hand-eye coordination to reach that close-window or exit-app button. Possibly not merely the One Second Rule, but one second without ever having the customer's complete attention.

So, coming back to the title of this section: where to start? The answer is to start with the customer. Maybe this is obvious, but in practice it's often a shift in focus for many retailers who are accustomed to start all planning processes from their assortment and/or brand (or most challenging of all, from their finance department).

3.2 Starting from the customer

So who is your customer? Most successful retailers have plenty of customers, and so the answer to this question is a broad spectrum. Even if your retail business occupies a specific niche, you can usually differentiate plenty of different customer sub-segments. One of the goals of personalisation (see **Chapter 24**) is to address each of these segments in slightly different ways. If you're already at that level of sophistication, the chances are you can skip this chapter! For the rest, this spectrum presents a problem. It simply isn't practical to instantly build experiences that suit every customer, and still pass the 1-second test I described above. Equally, if your typical customer purchase involves (say) 10 steps, and each step could take place on one of only two channels (e.g. in-store versus website), then that's $2^{10} = 1024$ customer journeys you need to consider. Most purchases involve more than 10 steps, and most Multichannel retailers have more than two touch-points. The numbers get completely out of hand.

The answer, and in fact current best practice, is to simplify the problem by resorting to stereotypes. There's some jargon: "Personas" - borrowed from advertising; and "UCD" – user centric design – because all disciplines need some three letter acronyms to confound the uninitiated. The simple idea is that if you get it right for your stereotypes, then it will probably be OK for the rest of your customers too. There's a practical side benefit to this approach too – it gets everybody talking in the same way, makes it easy to share priorities, and helps break down a lot of the communication barriers that might exist between, for example, your marketing and IT departments.

You could opt for a lengthy formal process to identify your personas, involving interviews with many of your employees and a large cross-section of your customers, with hopefully some very nice artwork as the output. In practice there's usually a much quicker=cheaper way: either you already know yourself (because you have good quality data available), or your store managers know (because they see these people every day). Just sit a group of store managers in a room and walk them through some basic questions about their customers – how old, what gender, what do they buy, what do they do for a living, is it the husband or wife that is making the decisions, who is paying, and so forth. It isn't particularly scientific, but the results are usually just as, if not more, valid than trawling through reams of analysis, and certainly just as useful at this early planning stage.

3.3 Creating Personas

A useful persona for the purposes of planning your multichannel proposition consists of just a few basic elements:

1. Basic demographics (age, gender, social class, income etc)

2. A "back-story" to bring them to life

3. A "mission statement" – what are they trying to do or (preferably!) buy. Clearly this should be representative of the typical reasons why your customers are usually looking to purchase

4. A relationship to your proposed channels (especially a relationship with the internet, or their mobile device)

5. A relationship to you, the retailer

Although it's a bit hypothetical without a real retail client, here's a brief, and <u>very much simplified</u> example:

Basic demographics: Chris is in his mid-forties, and lives with his wife and two teenage children in a suburb in a city in the English Midlands. He works as a freelance consultant, and enjoys a reasonable, if rather variable, income.

Back-story: Despite Chris's professional connections to technology and the internet in general, he never feels he knows quite as much about the topic as his teenage children appear to do! It seems like his daughter is the ultimate multi-channel shopper, while his son is permanently connected to his friends via a headset that has apparently been grafted to his skull. His wife, however, remains a determinedly reluctant user of technology.

Mission statement: As usual, Chris has failed to plan far enough ahead to buy a birthday present for his wife before an urgent client request takes him abroad on business. Over the years this has become a rather familiar scenario, and so his wife will understand that she'll get her main present later. However he would like to make sure a nice box of chocolates arrives on her actual birthday.

Relationship to your proposed channels: Chris travels extensively for his work, and is frequently away from home. Wherever he is in the world, however, he likes to stay in contact with his family on a daily basis. He is never without his smart-phone, and is an enthusiastic user of Skype. He will never stay in a hotel without a good internet connection, as online access is essential to him both personally and professionally.

Relationship to you, the retailer: Chris has never previously bought chocolates online. He has, of course, bought them on the high street, and therefore will probably start his research at a familiar name, expecting that in the UK a familiar high street store will also have a strong online offer.

While it's OK to give a single persona multiple mission-statements, you should resist the urge to create dozens of personas. In order for this technique to work effectively, everybody involved needs to be able to remember them all in meetings, and they need to come to life for everybody during discussions. Good advice is to create between 3 and 5 (maximum). Make sure you give each one an easy to remember name. The next step is to take a closer look at those mission statements, and break them down step-by-step. However this is the point where the customer meets the retailer, so before we go there, we need to take a closer look at how multichannel might change your basic retail proposition.

3.4 Top Takeaways

The One Second Rule is a benchmark for customer interaction.

Two paradigm shifts for a multichannel retailer to deal with are: customers have more power; everything happens faster.

Start from the customer... not assortment, brand or finance.

Begin by considering stereotypical customers: personas. Between 3 and 5 is the optimal number for initial planning purposes. Give them a memorable name!

A simple persona can be defined from five basic elements: basic demographics, back-story, mission statement, channel relationship, retailer relationship.

Chapter 4.   Introducing P.R.I.C.E. Differentiation

Differentiation for the multichannel retailer is not "special" in some way. The same rules of doing business still apply, and standard models for differentiation like Porter's quadrants are still just as relevant as ever. A list of the essential factors for a multichannel retailer to consider is made memorable by the acronym P.R.I.C.E.: Price, Range, Information, Convenience and Experience. This chapter will briefly introduce each topic, before the next five chapters consider each in turn in more depth.

4.1 Price

There has recently been a huge protest march in India by small family retailers against the government plans to allow multi-national chains to invest in majority owned retail outlets in what is currently a protected country market. The family retailers not unreasonably claim that the multi-nationals will have an unfair competitive advantage. Unfortunately, they are probably protesting against the wrong thing. If they really want to succeed in their objective they need to protest against the rollout of 3G mobile. Why? Because 3G mobile is how the great majority of all internet access is going to happen in India, and once you have internet access you have *price transparency*. In other words, you can check how much others are charging at the click of a few buttons.

Price transparency is often the biggest change that retailers have to come to terms with when considering their response to multichannel. Even in countries with relatively low internet penetration, it is already an issue in some categories (especially consumer electronics).

4.2 Range

Assortment is both an opportunity and an issue.

The opportunity exists in extending your range beyond what you can physically fit into your stores. In the more sophisticated multichannel retailers, this is not merely having a big range on your website, it's about making that big range available to customers in the stores as well. The endless aisle and the long tail are both key concepts to address.

The problem is that limited coverage in a particular category no longer cuts it. This is always a problem in limited-space retail, but is amplified by multichannel when it so easy for customers to just switch to another retailer's offer. The converse is also true however: offering a complete range drives sales, and multichannel makes it easier to offer a complete range. This is Amazon's original proposition summed up in one sentence, and look where it got them!

4.3 Information

On a very good retail website, only 3-5% of visits will result in a checkout. On a very good mobile site, you'll do very well indeed to convert 1% of visits. In a brick-and-mortar store, only some customers actually buy anything (offline conversion rates vary enormously: a few benchmarks include 31% in fashion in the US to over 85% in luxury retail in India). What are all those other visitors doing?

Online, half of them are just having a quick glance to see if you are relevant (remember that One Second Rule again) to their needs of the moment. The other half are there to do some research. Yes, it might just be price research, but it's quite likely to also be other research – product specification for example. Becoming an information destination build visits, builds brand recognition, builds sales across all your channels. It's also very difficult (=expensive) to do well. In a brick-and-mortar store, they are checking how the product looks and feels before going away to purchase it online (a phenomenon known as showrooming). It's still important to you that they chose your store as the showroom, because they are then more likely to subsequently make the purchase from you.

4.4 Convenience

Apart from price itself (but including *researching* price), Convenience is at the heart of why customers use multichannel.

Enjoying the Moscow traffic on the evening commuter run? Check the price of that laptop you've just spotted on an advertising hoarding. Suddenly remembered you've run out of coffee? Add it to your shopping list on your mobile. Want your box of chocolates to arrive exactly on your wife's birthday? Book the premium nominated-day delivery service on the website. Not in during the weekdays to receive that parcel? Click-and-collect to the nearest store, and pick it up at the weekend after dropping your son off at his football training.

4.5 Experience

Also known as Everything Else.

Obviously giving your customers a great experience goes without saying. What is important in multichannel retailing is that you also give your customers a *consistent* experience across all your touch-points. Internally you might be more or less organised into channels (see the discussions of organisation in **Chapter 22** and **Chapter 23**), but the customer is not going to understand this; they see you as one brand.

Just to pick a single, classic issue – you cannot refuse to accept returns from your website in your stores. Customers will return the stuff there anyway, whether you like it or not. Don't fight it, make it work seamlessly for them. Here's a quote from a top multichannel executive:

"It is not unusual for customers to view a product in-store and then to order it online for home delivery. But if they want to return it, they prefer to do so at the store because customers enjoy the physical experience of getting their money back." [11]

4.6 Top Takeaways

Multichannel retail differentiation can be described by the factors forming the acronym P.R.I.C.E.: price, range, information, convenience, experience.

---

[11] Laura Wade-Gery, executive director multichannel & eCommerce at Marks and Spencer, speaking the world retail congress, London, September 2012

Price transparency must be addressed by retailers in their response to multichannel.

Assortment (range) completeness is enabled by the endless aisle/long tail.

97% of website, 99% of smartphone, and a sizeable proportion of store visits do not lead directly to the checkout. Many of these customers are there for research (information) reasons.

Convenience is at the heart of why many customers choose multichannel.

Multichannel retailing experiences need to be consistent for the customer across all channels.

Chapter 5.   Price

5.1 Introduction: A Salzburg Nightmare

As an introduction to this topic, here's a case-study of a major retailer demonstrating how to get this issue extremely wrong:

Figure 11 - One Product, Two Prices! [12]

Two prices in *Figure 11*: an online price of €739 plus a further €9.90 for delivery; a store price *in Salzburg store only* of €699.

It's worth breaking this down step-by-step, just to illustrate some of the issues.

---

[12] Media Markt Austria website, screenshot taken in May 2010

5.1.1 Branding.

Figure 12 - Media Markt motto

Media Markt's slogan, emblazoned across their website, throughout their stores, and in all their advertising is approximately translated as "I'm not stupid". In other words, I know I'm getting a great deal from Media Markt. In the pre-internet days, before price transparency became commonplace, this might well have been true. Post internet, it still might be true, except that they went out of their way to carefully inform the customer that it was not true.

Firstly, the website appears to show two prices. So which is the "not stupid" price? Secondly, actually the website allowed you to change your designated store. And lo and behold, the prices in Salzburg are different to the prices in Vienna... or Innsbruck... or Graz... or you get the idea. So there could be 30+ prices for the same product? Which one is the stupid price now then?

5.1.2 Channel Conflict

Channel conflict is a topic we'll return to later (*Chapter 12*), but it's at the heart of what's gone wrong here. Media Markt stores are partially franchises, and the franchisees have made significant investment in their stores. They do *not* want to see themselves being undercut by the (head-office operated) website. Hence the excruciating attempts to have the website price higher than the store price.

5.1.3   Price comparison and transparency

Branded consumer electronics are particularly easy products to include in a price comparison website, or to price compare generally. Displaying a high online price means you'll have a high price on any price comparison site. Having a high price on a price comparison site means your customers will draw the obvious conclusion: you are expensive. It is particularly unfortunate if your slogan is "I'm not stupid" and you then demonstrate quite so explicitly to your customers that, if they were buying from you in the past, they probably were stupid. Reputational damage to your brand is not so easy to repair.

5.1.4   The world has changed

An alternative option, presumably rejected for the reasons mentioned the Channel Conflict point, would have been to have a lower price online, competitively positioned if not necessarily the lowest. The consequence would have been well-informed customers marching into stores and demanding the online price. The reality, of course, was that well-informed customers were already researching prices online. In the single currency zone of the EU, they could even easily extend their researches outside Austria if they so wished. These customers could already march into stores and demand an online price, or simply vote with their wallets and purchase from another retailer. Based on data recently published by Media Markt, it seems quite likely that the stores were quietly discounting their prices in a small way (2 -3% on average) when customers did so.[13]

But it cost them a CEO and a CFO to accept that the world really has changed, power has moved from the retailer to the customer, and it would be better to change than to die.

---

[13]http://www.metrogroup.de/internet/site/metrogroup/get/documents/met rogroup_international/corpsite/05_inrel/presentations/events-2011-07-26-MSH-Field-Trip.pdf

5.2 Strategic Options

Forewarned by this cautionary tale, we can explore some of the strategic options available.

5.2.1 Retreat from the high street

This is not quite as bizarre as it might sound. There are several credible instances of retailers simply deciding that retaining brick-and-mortar stores in the multichannel age was not going to work for them. Here's a quote from a fairly successful example, Shop Direct, a GBP 1.7 Bn business annually (around USD 2.5 Bn) with over 5M customers including the 3rd largest clothing and 5th largest non-food retailing brands in the UK:

"A 21st century business: Since 2005, we have transformed and modernised the entire business. We have <u>sold our stores</u> and merged the home shopping businesses to create the UK's leading online and home shopping retailer." [14] *[my underlining].*

Effectively they have turned themselves into a catalogue/phone-order/online pure-play, and done so fairly effectively. It has allowed them to strip costs out, and either compete on price or sell products where direct price competition is less of an issue. If you are pure-play in the first place, you probably already got there. If you are a successful mail-order or catalogue-based business, this is maybe not a good time to be opening stores.

5.2.2 Channel-based pricing

In the long run – and "long" here might be a matter of months, depending on the multichannel maturity stage of your country market – this is not sustainable. In a highly developed market like the UK or US, it's already probably not an option anyway. But there are plenty of examples of retailers who have managed to sustain pricing differently online versus offline for at least a short while, giving them a bit of breathing space to resolve the wider business model issues. A higher

---

[14] http://www.shopdirect.com/shop-direct/

price online, as Media Markt chose to try, is at best unorthodox, but a higher store price might be doable for a period.

Eventually customers will demand "One Retailer, One Price". Once this starts to happen, you have little option but to follow the money. However there are still ways to obfuscate the issue, which are generally accepted by consumers:

Channel specific promotions: Channel-based Promotions are usually considered acceptable, simply because customers get the concept rationally. In fact they may well be essential, particularly when choosing NOT to reflect store-based loss-leader promotions online. Put a stellar price for a highly desirable item up on a popular website, word will quickly go round the forums and social networks, and you'll get raped. And on a website, it won't generate as much in terms of cross-sell or beneficial incidental footfall that you might see in brick-and-mortar. People will just buy the cheap item that you're losing money on.

Shipping Fees: Recover some of the lost margin via fees, especially Delivery Fees. Delivery fees are a complex topic, and the subject of a separate section (see section **18.2**). Other fees are more dubious, and although that doesn't seem to stop budget airlines, I can't think of an example where it's been successfully sustained in straight retail.

Just to reiterate, this is probably only a temporarily viable strategy, but if you are operating in a less developed market, then it may well work for you for a short period. Once 3G mobile and smartphones are a reality for a significant proportion of your customers, then the showrooming factor comes into play. Customers in your stores will check online *while they are in your stores* and validate the prices. There have been some desperate attempts to prevent this behaviour – Best Buy in the US for example, tried proprietary barcodes for some of their higher ticket items to stop customers scanning generic bar-codes with their smartphone – but they are destined to fail. More sensible retailers are taking the route of accepting they can't beat this behaviour, and offering their customers free in-store Wi-Fi as a service instead (see the Digital Stores section *13.3*).

5.2.3   Be the cheapest!

If you had a price advantage before the days of price transparency, then now you have a PRICE ADVANTAGE: great news, stop reading this book now, and get out there marketing yourself like crazy. Otherwise, take a hard look at what this option would mean for your business. If you are fortunate enough to have the buying power, then you have been given the ammunition to squeeze the life out of your suppliers (sometimes literally, unfortunately). Otherwise, of course it means reduced gross margins. This is a fairly horrible thought, but it's much more horrible if you are forced into it reactively by your customers and competitors than if you plan for it, and take all your stakeholders with you on the journey.

Our useful Media Markt case study also illustrates a retailer that has now decided to address this challenge proactively. *Figure 13* summarises the plan in their published investor relations presentation. In summary, they believe their stores are already discounting in practice due to online price pressure, and therefore that they have already absorbed some of this in reduced effective margins. They plan then to reduce margins by a further 2-3% to retain price perception compared to larger/credible online brands, which they will compensate for via various cost savings. Separately they will also continue a two brand strategy for now. Only time will tell if this is going to work, but at least the issue has been tackled explicitly head-on and a strategic plan put into action.

Figure 13 - Planning for reduced gross margins[15]

5.2.4 Don't sell products that customers can price-compare

Simple? Well not necessarily. If you have non-comparable products, especially something like own-branded fashion, then it probably is simple. But even in some of the war-zones like consumer electronics there are various options being explored by multichannel retailers. The reason consumer electronics is a war-zone in the first place is that, in any country with reasonable consumer-protection legislation, a customer can always be certain that if they purchase a Widget 2013GTi, that's exactly what they are going to get, no matter who they purchase it from. So they may as well buy from the cheapest outlet. The retailer is merely acting as a supply-conduit from brand manufacturer to end-customer, retaining a service-fee for the transaction, and getting no more long-term value from the transaction than the credit-card provider who processes the customer's payment.

---

[15]http://www.metrogroup.de/internet/site/metrogroup/get/documents/met rogroup_international/corpsite/05_inrel/presentations/events-2011-07-26-MSH-Field-Trip.pdf

The challenge for the retailer is to transform the transaction in some way.

One option is to completely change the concept of the transaction in the first place – to stop it being just a supply-conduit/service-fee transaction – by adding value along the way, for example by providing set-up, configuration, knowledge, support or other services. This is an element of the strategy being pursued, for example, by Dixons Retail (PC World) in the UK. Japan's Yamada Denki offers the same idea in a different flavour.

Another option is to change the Widget so that you have an exclusive Widget 2013GTk while everybody else only has the 2013GTi. Basically the same product, slightly different specification, no longer price comparable (in theory anyway). Many branded goods manufacturers are rapidly waking up to this issue and supporting their retailer clients in these endeavours. If you are a retailer in an even slightly vulnerable category, then putting in place such a long-term strategic co-operation with your brands is strongly recommended, even if you yourselves have no immediate Multichannel plans. (Other brands try to avoid supplying in the first place to retailers who might discount, especially luxury brands. I once did an engagement with a luxury jewellery retailer planning to go online who found their plans seriously hampered by non-cooperative brands. Adidas/Reebok have recently announced that authorised dealers will be banned from selling their products on Amazon or eBay marketplaces, citing brand-devaluation arguments[16]). Even the most basic steps like offering the 6Gb of memory option while everybody else has the 4Gb or 8Gb are a start.

Still another possibility is to take a lead from mobile phone service providers, and group products into bundles that prevent the customer directly comparing prices, for example as a product + extended warranty option.

---

[16] See for example http://www.e-commercefacts.com/news/2012/06/adidas-dislikes-ebay-and-/index.xml

One last choice is some kind of price maintenance collaboration, either official or unofficial, within your market. These come with a high risk even where legal. You may well be able to obstruct legislation preventing this kind of behaviour. You are unlikely to be able to stop customers remembering that it's not called the World Wide Web for no reason, and just switching to purchasing from overseas websites. A current high-profile example is Australia, where the issue is exacerbated by sales tax that does not apply to goods shipped in from overseas until they are of significant value. The UK government has recently moved this threshold right down virtually nil partly as a result of tax-haven pure-plays undercutting local retailers (and reducing the government tax-take as a consequence), but it hasn't really eased the price competition, just moved the bar a bit.

5.2.5 Two Brands

Not every customer is an internet-loving, comparison-trawling, price-obsessed shopper. And even in countries where this appears to be the case, it doesn't happen overnight. Yes, your younger customers may well live online, but younger customers don't necessarily have much buying power on average. The Rise of the Silver Surfer (i.e. older people becoming heavy internet users) is a phenomenon that takes some time to happen in every country.

Russia is a reasonable semi-developed example. Multichannel in Russia could reasonably be described as relatively immature. Only around 1% of retail sales are non-store in Russia (compared to over 10% in the UK[17]), but internet and broadband penetration is rising rapidly in the major cities, to almost 70% in Moscow and St Petersburg.[18] How is this 70% divided?

---

[17] UK Office of National Statistics.
[18] TNS Web Index, Russia

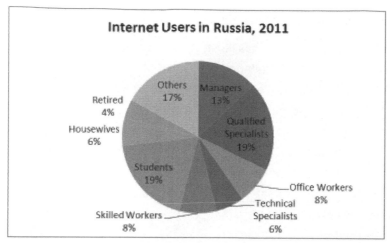

Figure 14 - distribution of internet users (aged > 12) in Russia
2011[19]

As Figure 14 shows, only 4% of internet users (aged > 12) are retired, and yet 15% of the population (aged > 12) are over 65.[20] There remains a significant segment for whom the internet is still a rumour.

In a market like Russia, a two brand strategy might well be a reasonable option. One online pure-play brand for the young price-comparers, another multichannel brand with the emphasis on stores and service for the rest. Once again our Media Markt case-study illustrates the point. Even in a market as developed as Germany, the company still believes a two brand strategy is feasible, and has purchased an online pure-play Redcoon.de (let's hope they don't try roll out this brand-name in any English speaking markets!) as part of its Multichannel strategy.

If this is an appropriate option in your local market, then the important thing is to plan your exit strategy at the same time. Eventually your customers will become more multichannel aware, the Silver Surfers will come floating in, and you'll have to converge the brands (as Dixons Retail plc are now doing in the UK for example).

---

[19] TNS Web Index, 2011
[20] CIA World Factbook, www.cia.gov

5.2.6 Don't Compete on Price

As I hope this chapter has illustrated, competing on price in a price-transparent world is challenging at best. If possible, make plans to shift into less price-driven product ranges. If you can't avoid selling products that customers can price compare, you can always choose not to worry too much if you lose a few sales due to price comparison, and focus on those customers for whom price is not the biggest issue.

Don't let this happen by drifting into it. Price transparency is coming to a country near you right now, so if your strategy is not to compete on price while remaining active in price-sensitive categories, plan strategically for it. Expect to see sales volumes reduce, aim to see profitability increase. Consider what this means for your stores estate. And if price is not your differentiator, then make sure something else is!

5.3 Top Takeaways

The challenge of price transparency requires a planned strategic response. It won't go away, ignoring it is unacceptable without an active plan for reduced sales volumes, and artificial workarounds are unsustainable.

The benefits of a price advantage will be magnified by multichannel.

Showrooming – customers using stores as a place to inspect products before then buying them via the cheapest channel (often online) – cannot be prevented.

The world-wide web means that customers can also shop across borders for standardised products; single country cartels are easily bypassed.

Channel based pricing may be a temporary option, but is unsustainable in the long term, because it is inconsistent with offering customers a seamless multichannel experience. Channel based promotions, however, are generally acceptable.

Unique specification products increase in relative importance: own brands, distinct specifications, product bundles. Supplier partners should be engaged to help.

A two brand strategy is possible in countries/markets which divide sharply into internet literate and illiterate customer segments, especially where buying power remains significantly offline and Silver Surfers are not yet common.

A few retailers have elected to simply retreat from brick-and-mortar completely.

Chapter 6.   Range

6.1 Kompetenz

Run this nice German word through Google Translate, and you'll get four very relevant words as the English definition: "capability, authority, competence, jurisdiction."

"Jurisdiction" is the odd man out, but still worth some quick discussion. This is the World-Wide Web: put a product up for sale on a website, and in principle anybody from anywhere can try to buy it. They may fail for two basic hygiene reasons: a) you don't offer a delivery service to their location; b) you block payments from methods registered in their country (probably for fraud-prevention reasons – see **Chapter 20**). Otherwise, you can theoretically sell to them.

The important question is then: do you have contractual permission from your supplier to sell this product in that location? If your products are music or film or similar, then the answer is almost certainly no. If your products are premium branded items, then the answer is maybe still no. Even if your products are "standard" products, it is extremely sensible to take the precaution of changing your supplier Terms & Conditions to explicitly give you permission to sell these products via non-store channels. This should be a basic first step for any brick-and-mortar retailer planning to add virtual channels – review all your supplier contracts, and change them if needed. In fact if you are brick-and-mortar retailer who is even thinking about possibly going multichannel sometime in the distant future, this is a very useful foundation to address now. Changing contracts or terms and conditions is much more easily done gradually over time as contracts naturally come up for renewal.

Basic legal issues being safely taken care of, let's return to "capability, authority, competence." Bookshops are usually nice places. You can get a coffee and a cake, browse through hundreds or thousands of books to your heart's content. The staff are generally a world-away from the typical supermarket checkout clerk, helpfully passionate about books and reading. And yet, even in its pre-Kindle, books-only days, Amazon started to vacuum up their market. The most basic reason: on Amazon you can find every book currently in print, and with the arrival of the Amazon Marketplace, almost every book that has ever been in print. When it comes to books, Amazon has capability, authority, competence.

The Amazon/books story is an extreme case of a well-documented phenomenon when multichannel hits a category. Kompetenz has always been a relevant consideration for retailers. Those secondary categories have always been slightly unconvincing to customers, but worthwhile sticking with either because they're reasonably profitable in their own right, or because they help complete your assortment overall. Multichannel simply moves the bar up: secondary categories are no longer slightly unconvincing, they're now completely unconvincing. And many retailers are seeing their secondary category sales drop off dramatically as a consequence. It's part of the shift in power away from the retailer towards the customer.

I don't want to bombard this section with evidential data points in support of the above assertions, but just take a look at the annual results for almost any retailer in a market with significant multichannel players, and it will include phrases like "focussing on our core categories". A telling quote from the CEO of one of the biggest players:

"As we look forward, I think our larger stores will have a bit more food space, a little bit less general merchandise space, a bit more clothing space."[21]

This quote nicely highlights the secondary category decisions that most multichannel players face, or that other retailers have to tackle in the face of multichannel competitors. Get out of the category, reinforce the category, move the category to a more appropriate channel? Just don't do nothing and hope the problem will go away – the problem won't, but you probably will (see Woolworths UK or Neckermann Germany as a few of many examples). So how do you reinforce the category, or move it to a more appropriate channel,

---

[21] Tesco CEO Philip Clarke, interview 3rd October 2012

within the reasonable constraints of store space? The answer lies in the Endless Aisle.

6.2 The Endless Aisle

At its simplest, the Endless Aisle just means offering a fully complete range in a particular category. Amazon and books is the obvious example again. Once you step outside the boundaries of store space-planning constraints, the only limits lie in your supply chain and buying. We'll discuss supply chain issues in **Chapter 20**, so for now let's just assume that you can plan a category unconstrained by anything except overall coherence and margin.

The outcome of such a category plan is inevitable: you just range everything your customers might ever want. This chapter is about differentiation, so from a customer perspective, what you aim to become is a go-to destination for the category. For the online pure-play retailers this is so easy to do that customers now come to expect it. If you can't offer a complete range, your sales will suffer badly. There is a slightly bizarre corollary to exploit as well: many retailers find that increasing the size of their range in a category drives sales, not of the extended range, but of the core items. It's a bit like those corner-stores that display five cheap brands of blended whisky on the shelves plus a ridiculously expensive premium single malt in a locked glass cabinet. No-one buys the premium malt, but people feel better about buying the cheap brands because it's there.

For the true multichannel retailer, with both brick-and-mortar stores and online sales channels, there are now some nice options. In your stores, you can focus on core categories, on take-away categories, and on categories which don't work well online (e.g. light-bulbs is a nice example of a category that is tricky online for a whole host of reasons). The big opportunity then lies in those secondary, space-constrained, potentially threatened categories. Suddenly they are no longer space-constrained. To make this work well, of course, your customers have to be able to order that extended range in store, and they also have to be able to pick it up in store.

Enabling this kind of elastic store is what drives basics like click-and-collect, but also drives the development of in-store ordering points and kiosks. NB in most categories, standalone kiosks unsupported by staff do NOT work; I've been involved in a few failed pilots. This is another thing Apple currently gets right – the staff assist you to order. There is a challenging implication to all this: your store-staff have to be familiar with your non-store range and able to explain and sell it to customers.

In the UK and US, it's already starting to drive another strategic shift: shrinking the average size of stores and the overall store estate. An extreme version of this concept is now being piloted by some retailers in the UK, although it's probably going to take a few iterations to get it right: the stock-less store. We'll come back to this again when we take a look a Digital Stores later on (**Chapter 13**).[22]

In some markets the availability of decent quality retail space is an issue (Ukraine for example). As/when customers become educated to understand this kind of elastic-store type offer, and/or store staff can be given good enough tools to explain it to customers, there may be less challenges in finding quality locations, hopefully reducing overall costs significantly while allowing greater overall coverage of the country.

6.3 Top Takeaways

Kompetenz - capability, authority, competence, jurisdiction – is essential to demonstrate in a multichannel category.

Multichannel can have the effect of making primary categories relatively stronger, secondary categories relatively weaker.

Endless Aisles allow retailers to plan assortments unconstrained by store space.

The Long Tail of the range must be available on all channels, including stores.

---

[22] See for example http://www.bbc.co.uk/news/uk-scotland-scotland-business-15411541 covering House of Fraser Aberdeen pilot store

Elastic Stores offer additional options: reduced space or stock-less stores. However customers must be able to order and/or collect non-stock products in the store.

Supplier contracts should be amended as soon as possible to permit products to be sold via non-store channels.

Chapter 7.   Information

7.1 A two-way trade

99% of smart-phone visitors, 97% of website visitors, and most likely well over 50% of brick-and-mortar store visitors don't buy anything when they visit you. So what use are they to you? Well the chances are they're there to gather information. For at least half of them, that information is probably just price.[23] For the other half they're looking for something more. Seeking alternative products, ratings & reviews, detailed specifications, inspiration, how-to, are a few amongst a multitude of possible objectives. The question when considering your differentiation approach is whether to service any of these objectives, and if so, whether you can extract any value from the customer for doing so.

Here's just one basic dilemma (although caveat emptor here: the current deluge of mobile-related statistics, mainly from those with a vested interest, can be used to "prove" just about any plausible argument). In a recent survey of smart-phone owners in France, Sweden and Germany[24], 71% had used their smart-phone to research products, and 32% had done so in the previous week. Great, better get a mobile site then. But 90% of smart-phone owners who used their mobile *while in a store* to research products were looking at *somebody else's site*.[25] Scrap the mobile site again.

Speaking personally, for me the ultimate nightmare customer experience is that of buying a used-car from a showroom forecourt. It seems like every word I utter gives the salesman more and more information about me that allows him to exploit my ignorance of

---

[23] Tesco CEO Philip Clarke at the World Retail Congress, September 2012: "Over half of visits to our Tesco.com website are to check prices - and this is our food site, not our general merchandise site"

[24]

http://www.tradedoubler.com/pagefiles/25098/tradedoubler_shopping_on_mobile_oct2012_uk.pdf

[25] See for example http://www.slideshare.net/kkrossing/2011-mobile-retail-infographics

motoring matters in general, and then use it sell me something that I probably don't really need for more than I ought to be paying. A key reason why customers do so much research online in the first place is to avoid being put at the same information disadvantage as me looking at used-cars. In a less malign way, deciding to service your customers' information needs is similar to that second-hand car salesman's patter. Everything your customer does tells you something about them. Even the simple act looking at a product tells you the customer is interested in that product, and possibly in other similar products, related items, accessories etc.

There is a two-way trade. The customer tells you something about themselves. You then have the opportunity to use this information to tell the customer something about yourself which will be "beneficial" to the customer. There are a series of potential investment decisions to consider:

Reference data: should you invest in providing detailed factual information, in the expectation of some knock-on benefit: short-term such as rapidly converting that customer or gathering data about them; longer-term, such as customer brand-loyalty or even simply returning to us a bit later to make a purchase?

Active data: should you invest in actively seeking to exploit customers' use of this reference information, which in turn causes them to disclose information about themselves which you can exploit to advantage?

Personalisation: can you take this one step further and change your proposition or behaviour on a customer-by-customer basis, based on the information each customer discloses?

Multichannel reuse: can you carry the information provided by customers on one channel across to our other channels (especially from online into brick-and-mortar)?

Customer participation: should your customers contribute to the information, for example via ratings and reviews, or social networks?

Destination information: should you invest in providing information over-and-above the merely factual, for example in how-to guides?

7.2 Reference data

In the later chapters on Product Data Management (**Chapter 15** and **Chapter 19**), I'll develop this argument much further. Let's just assert here that basic reference data about your products is a wonderful thing. It's the foundation of your online channels – every website needs to display its products! It can also be the foundation of many other competitive advantages in brick-and-mortar operations: better informed sales staff, better wrap-rates in call-centres, lower returns rates (it's surprising how many fully-functioning electrical items are returned because neither customers nor staff knew how to switch them on), to name just a few.

But reference data is also very expensive to capture. The industry benchmark figure is that capturing even basic good quality product information plus a reasonable quality image requires an average of 25 man-minutes per SKU. Or put another way, 4000 SKUs requires one *FTE-year* of work. And it's quite a skilled job, so that FTE-year is probably an expensive graduate FTE-year (product data maintenance is a typical first-job-after-college type of role, so watch out if you're reading this as part of your course – you have been warned!).

In less developed online markets, many online pure-plays do fairly well without ever really tackling this task properly. They have a buying-price/cost-base advantage, they exploit this price advantage for all it's worth, and that is sufficient for now. Sustaining this advantage as the market around them catches up, however, usually requires them to bite the bullet and make the effort.[26] In very developed markets, other

---

[26] Just as one typical example, see www.rozetka.com.ua; before you object that you don't read Russian, auto-translate is the main plus point of using Google Chrome as a web-browser. Actually I'm hoping that you do read Russian, as Russia is a big potential new market for the services of people like me!

online-pureplays still don't make a great job of it.[27] Amazon's data about many consumer electronics items could best be described as average. Amazon in the US, however, has found another way to provide this data, and it's called Best Buy.

Some basic data is unavoidable. It's pretty difficult to sell apparel without telling the customer what size the garment is, and if you want to sell it online, showing high quality imagery is a must (some displaying the item on a real model: cut out pictures alone don't cut it). If your product is an Own Brand, then you have no choice but to be the reference data source for it. For the rest, there is a serious commercial decision to take: are you the right player to be the reference data source for this category of data online? If you are, can you translate this into sales, or would it be better to leave this to the competition, or better still, the manufacturer? How much data is sufficient to be the reference? Do you really need to capture every item from the back-of-label data (**Figure 15**) in order to give the customer the experience they require? It comes back to your customers and personas again: what do they need for the missions you've defined for them? Never forget that multichannel retail is customer-centric first, product-centric second.

---

[27] Compare these two pages for the same product, one from the US and one from the Ukraine, on these two website. For example: http://www.amazon.com/Panasonic-DMC-FZ150K-Digital-Camera-Optical/dp/B005HQ50SO and http://rozetka.com.ua/panasonic_lumix_dmc_fz150_black/p169041/. Which is better?

Figure 15 – for one loaf of bread, 43 data points are needed?[28]

There's not much of that two-way trade-off in basic passive reference data. OK, the customer has told you they are interested, you've responded by asserting your authority as a source in this area. Hopefully the customer responds to this assertion in the same way as they respond to Kompetenz in assortment.

7.3 Active Data

By looking at the reference information, the customer has told you they are interested in one of your products. How do you actively respond? By trying to sell them something else. Amazon allegedly shared the statistic that in 2006, cross-sells accounted for 35% of all their sales. Google for this statistic and you'll find it endlessly repeated, but you may well struggle to find the original source. And in any case, Amazon represents a special case, particularly in books and music. Amazon also has something else that most retailers don't have: the data on a huge number of very similar shopping visits for highly homogeneous products to analyse statistically to construct their cross-sells.

This isn't to say that cross-selling doesn't work. Most studies imply a sales uplift of somewhere in the 3-5% range. But once again there's

---

[28] Tesco.com, collage of screenshots, January 2011

an investment to make. Either you've got to analyse the data if you've got it, and possibly then re-present it to your customers via some software, or you've got to create and maintain it manually. Automation doesn't necessarily work even for Amazon. Take this example, which only took me a couple of minutes to find on their US site (*Figure 16*):

Figure 16 – the USB connected pressure cooker?[29]

How has this error occurred? It has happened because Amazon is actively exploiting information provided by customers. When a lot of customers do something, the inferences drawn will be statistically valid. When a very small number of customers do something, the inferences can end up being bizarre. Amazon doesn't make too many mistakes like this because their huge data volumes of fairly similar carts help prevent it. Most other retailers end up maintaining/cleaning this data semi-manually; if you sell smaller volumes of bigger ticket items you may have no other option. It is one of the areas where multichannel retailers have a distinct advantage over their pure-play cousins: the skills and knowledge already exist in the merchandising teams. A good percentage of the "customers who bought this also bought that" data you see online is probably partially faked, while the

---

[29] Collated screen-shot from Amazon.com, October 2012

majority of alleged "best sellers" should be regarded with deep suspicion.

It probably is worth doing, but do make the business-case explicitly first, based on some reasonable estimated upside. There's a lot of data maintenance required and/or some expensive software needed, for an upside which in one recent study might be as low as 0.2% of profits.[30] I'd suggest you use 3% as a planning/business-case benchmark, but beware that the effectiveness is notoriously difficult to actually measure, especially in true multichannel where the customer might see the cross-sell on a website, but then go buy it in store later. (Note to analytics enthusiasts: it's not enough to measure A/B-tested click-through rates, you need to measure whether these clicks result in overall more *net profitable* customer shopping carts).

7.3.1 Multichannel reuse

Surprisingly few multichannel retailers seem to take this customer/data-based learning back into their stores. Cross-sells which work online, also work in store. Do put the top cross-selling online items next to each other on your shelf planograms. Do make this information available to your store staff if you operate the kind of stores where staff are actively selling to customers on the shop-floor; tell your staff what works online, because it will work offline too – your customers have told you so.

7.3.2 Personalisation

This topic is covered in detail in **Chapter 24**. It's the next logical step on the journey. In the "customers who looked at X finally bought Y" offers described above, every customer who looks at X will be suggested Y. Personalisation considers information gleaned about the individual customer to decide whether it would be better to suggest Z to that particular individual instead.

The standard formula "customers who bought this also bought" is worth further inspection. There is a reason why retailers don't say "we

---

[30]See for example http://econsultancy.com/uk/blog/8632-up-selling-is-20-times-more-effective-than-cross-selling-online

suggest you also think about." Customers trust other customers much more than they trust retailers. Which is why the next section is...

7.4 Customer Generated Information

Ratings and reviews drive sales. In 2005.

OK, that isn't really fair, ratings and reviews still drive sales, and back in the happy days of 2005-6, when it was possible to make presentations about Web 2.0 being the future, some quite credible, reasonably well controlled studies were published, showing plausible average sales uplifts in the 12-30% range. Ignore any hype about them driving 300% increases. Yes, they maybe could drive a 300% increase for a well-reviewed top-selling line. But reviews aren't all good, not every product is a top-seller, and 12-30% is still a great average. The market leaders in this space currently claim average uplifts in the 15-25% range.[31]

But... the internet is full of reviews. By the time most customers come to buy it, every branded product has already been reviewed, multiple times on multiple sites. Customers shopping on any channel, including brick-and-mortar, will have read at least one review[32], probably several, or if they haven't already will read a review on their smart-phone whilst standing in your store checking out the product. (One minor mystery, actually, is why so few brick-and-mortar stores seem to acknowledge this reality and display highlights of positive ratings and reviews on their shelf-edges.)

If you have own-branded products that won't get reviewed elsewhere, if your target customers generally don't have access to other review sites, if your customers' native language and education is likely to make it difficult for them go elsewhere for the information, if

---

[31] For example, see www.reevoo.com, who claim an uplift of +18%; no endorsement or otherwise implied

[32] For example see this study by PWC claiming that 88% of all US shoppers research online first, and still 73% even in more challenging categories like fashion, footwear and health (http://www.pwc.com/en_US/us/retail-consumer/publications/assets/pwc-us-multichannel-shopping-survey.pdf)

internet penetration is still quite low in your country or region so it's still relatively new for customers, then implement them.

Otherwise, yes, your online channels probably need to display reviews and ratings. But have a serious look at whether or not you have to manage them, or whether to just syndicate them in. If you are going to do them yourself, you really have to drive your customers to post them. There needs to be sufficient critical mass of them to make it worthwhile for customers to stay on your site and read them in preference to looking someplace else. You have to follow up with your customers to get them to rate and post reviews. You have to moderate them (check them for appropriateness). Soliciting them may be great reactivation email marketing campaigns, or it may be a costly pain in the neck. Generating sufficient critical mass needs to be a KPI in its own right. There is a real cost to operating and managing them, potentially with very little readership. That's not to say don't do it, just take a proper look at the options and the business case first. Do it very well, like Amazon, and you immediately become an information destination, the go-to place for customers considering your categories. Do it poorly and you look limp, and it will actually cost you sales: it damages that Kompetenz differentiation you've worked so hard to demonstrate.

Operationally, by the way, don't omit the other side of the story. One negative review doesn't matter. Multiple negative reviews are telling you something (usually. There are instances of coordinated bad reviews, one example being teenage PC gamers protesting at effective software copy protection techniques, which – gasp – meant they might actually have to pay for the software, coordinating negative ratings and reviews on Amazon). Monitor reviews of your assortment. If it's an own-brand product, do something to fix it, and tell your customers you did so; listening-to-you messages are generally good marketing. If it isn't, get it on clearance before everybody else does. I realise this is an isolated data point, but the suggestion in one study that 80% of people changed purchase decision after seeing negative reviews seems intuitively reasonable, and should be a real call-to-action.[33]

Customers trust each other more than they trust you the retailer, but they trust their friends even more. Informal reviews via social networks are very strong influencers, but of course they are pretty difficult for retailers to do much about. There's no point in trying to fight it, so you may as well make it easy (hence all those "share this" buttons), monitor where you can, respond if possible.

7.5 Help and Advice

One of my favourite websites of all time is Blue Nile[34], although sorry, Blue Nile, I've never actually bought anything from you; as they reported earnings of $16.9M in 2011 on sales of $340M[35], it doesn't look like they've suffered too badly from the lack of my personal custom. As you might guess from the name, they sell jewellery with a particular focus on diamonds. Not something that most people, even those who (unlike me!) can afford it, buy every day, or in general know too much about. Recognising that this ignorance is an opportunity to attract customers who might be intimidated by displaying their lack of knowledge face-to-face in an expensive store, their customer experience successfully focusses on educating the customer throughout the journey (*Figure 17*).

Figure 17 - Education at Blue Nile

This is an example of one company which has focussed on help and advice as a differentiator. OK it's an online pure-play, and yes

---

[33]Survey by Cone Inc, presented for example at http://www.marketingpilgrim.com/2011/08/80-percent-of-shoppers-change-purchase-decision-based-on-negative-reviews-research.html
[34] www.bluenile.com
[35] Investor.bluenile.com

diamonds are a slightly special category. But Blue Nile have evidently succeeded in translating education into (profitable) sales.

The same concept can be translated into a true multichannel retailer too. Anglo-French DIY retailer Kingfisher (Castorama / B&Q core brands, with 955 stores in 8 countries) has invested heavily in "how to do the job" videos (and other content) which are a key feature of its websites (*Figure 18*).

Figure 18 - Advice from Castorama[36]

The roll-out of advice and help is a key reporting target, tracked in its annual shareholder report, and associated with a stated KPI measure of like-for-like sales growth.[37] More than a hundred multi-lingual videos represent a serious investment, and nobody does that (and tracks in their annual report) without a solid business case. The expectation is not that it will drive specifically *online* sales (DIY is a category with relatively low online penetration) but that it will drive *overall* sales growth.

Last word goes to another pure-play, Asos, currently emerging as a possible Amazon of branded fashion online:

"2011/12 has been a stellar year for ASOS Magazine... and the December 2011 cover shoot with Jessica Chastain achieved 50 million global viewers."[38]

7.6 Top Takeaways

Multichannel customers visit all sales-channels first for information/research and only second to make purchases.

---

[36] Collage from castorama.pl, castorama.fr, diy.com
[37] See Kingfisher plc annual report and accounts 2011/12
[38] Asos plc, annual reports for the year ended 31 March 2012

Customer research activity via online channels is also a source of data about the customer which can be exploited by the retailer.

There are a series of investment decisions to make in: reference data, active data, personalisation, multichannel reuse, customer participation, destination information.

Product reference data is a key enabler, but is expensive to capture. It is important to make a business case for becoming an information reference source over and above the minimum basic data necessary to sell products online.

Cross-selling is a proven sales driver on online channels, but the benefit is more difficult to measure for multichannel retailers where the ultimate sale might take place in brick-and-mortar store.

"Customers who did X also did Y" merchandising is highly sensitive to data volumes. With low volumes, significant manual maintenance may be required.

For online channels, there is a big overlap between exploiting customer research activity, cross-selling, and personalisation.

Ratings and reviews are also proven sales drivers. A decision is required whether it is appropriate to collect and moderate them yourself, or whether to syndicate this task to save costs and exploit a wider pool.

Information on online channels, such as how-to guides, can drive sales across all channels, including brick-and-mortar.

Feedback from customers online, such as ratings and reviews, can be reused in brick-and-mortar.

Chapter 8.   Convenience

RAMASSAGE *GRATUIT*
EN MAGASIN EN **UNE HEURE**

Figure 19 - Free pick-up in store in 1 hour[39]

8.1 The Future of Shopping?

Back in the happy days of the tech bubble, the internet was going to change the way we shopped forever. Of course it has, but not quite in the way that most of the bubble hype envisaged. Stores are not obsolete (although some retailers now have too many – see later **Chapter 13**). Customers do not merely want to sit at their PCs buying and then hang around waiting for a delivery. Convenience is still a crucial motivator for customers, and a convenience advantage is still a key differentiator, but the key learning since the hyped-up days of 2000-1 is that convenience is defined not by the retailer but by the customer. It's a standard lesson in another form: multichannel has shifted power from the retailer to the consumer. The customer chooses what is convenient for *himself/herself*, the retailer needs to offer them options. And convenience is very difficult to "force" on customers, and extremely difficult to get them to pay a premium for: time-is-money may apply to airline travel, but it doesn't necessarily apply to shopping.

As online retailing starts up in a particular market, it is often able to offer a genuine step-change in convenience for customers. More transparent and (often) faster delivery than traditional mail-order, for example; stores which are indeed effectively open 7 x 24; grocery shopping without the toddler in tow. If you are in a country where online/multichannel is still relatively new, it is more than likely that a convenience advantage will help drive sales. See for example this delivery promise picked at random from my recent experience (**Figure 20**).

---

[39] www.lasource.ca, October 2012

Обычно если вы разместили заказ до 15:00 — мы доставим его в тот же день. В любом случае во время заказа наши менеджеры сразу согласуют с вами время доставки.

Figure 20 - Order by 15:00 and we'll deliver the same day[40]

What is certain in every country is that a convenience *disadvantage* will prevent sales. Perhaps the clearest illustration of this idea can be seen in a recent new option from Amazon (**Figure 21**).

Figure 21 - Amazon Locker: collection point, London Tube station

It is NOT convenient for many customers to wait at home for deliveries during working-hours, or to go to a distant courier-company's offices; they want their good at a place they can reach, at a time they can reach it. In this space, pure-play retailers are at a clear differentiation disadvantage compared to the true multichannel retailer.

8.2 The Empire Strikes Back

"Our product mix lends itself to a multi-channel offer as customers often want further advice, a demonstration or fitting. Online

---

[40] http://rozetka.com.ua/payments-and-deliveries/

purchasing patterns reflect this, with <u>*86% of sales on Halfords.com*</u> *reserved and then collected from a store.*"[41] *[my underlining].*

Clearly collect-in-store is not the only way in which truly multichannel retailers can have an advantage over their pure-play opponents, but it is probably one of the most obvious. It also represents a true step-change to multichannel thinking, and is discussed in depth in **Chapter 26**. The first response of existing brick-and-mortar retailers to the challenge of internet pure-plays is often to simply open an internet channel themselves. This offers them all the disadvantages of their store estate – most basically a higher cost-base – without any of its corresponding advantages: their online offer is no better than the pure-plays and probably (due to lack of competence or focus) worse. It is multiple-channel where multichannel is required.

The "post-checkout" phases of customer purchase self-evidently offer many opportunities for true multichannel retailers to differentiate themselves, especially against pure-plays. Interestingly, and at this stage speculatively, the steady development of mobile/smartphone as a channel, may well offer opportunities "pre-checkout". So far, mobile take-up of retail in countries with both the infrastructure and the smartphone wielding customer base is very significant, but conversion remains a challenge. Conversion rates on smartphones (as distinct from tablets, which offer a completely different customer experience – much nearer to a traditional PC - and should not be blended in statistically) are relatively poor.[42] Where are these customers converting then? Well, online via other devices or in-store, obviously. Capturing those missing conversions should be a key target for any retailer operating in a smartphone intensive country. For example online, one excellent way to achieve this is a shopping cart which the customer can add-to via mobile but then retrieve later

---

[41] Annual Report & Accounts 2012, Halfords plc

[42] There are lots of conflicting data points. A reasonable recent example study (www.monetate.com) has PC conversion at 3.34%, tablet at 3.17%, but smart-phone at only 1.09% - importantly this study does not bundle tablets in as "mobile"

on their PC to complete the keystroke intensive/security conscious checkout process. In-store, sophisticated multichannel retailers are realising they can't fight customers with smart-phones, much better to offer them free Wi-Fi, and use it as a differentiator and marketing channel. See the chapter on mobile for more discussion (**Chapter 25**).

Such concepts begin to overlap ever more with the final differentiation heading, Experience.

Figure 22 - Making the customer feel in control[43]

8.3 Top Takeaways

Convenience is defined by the customer, not the retailer.

Brick-and-mortar stores can offer a major convenience advantage over online pure-plays. For example, UK retailer Halfords sees 86% of its online orders collected in store, because customers value the follow-up services they can get there.

Online pure-play retailers need to counter this. For example, Amazon has introduced Amazon Locker as part of its response.

Smartphones are convenient for customers but conversion rates are currently poor. Retailers need to ensure that a seamless multichannel customer experience drives non-converting smartphone customers to conveniently convert via other channels.

(Mobile is covered in depth in Chapter 25. Click-and-collect is covered in depth in Chapter 26.)

---

[43] Marks & Spencer, October 2012

Chapter 9.   Experience

"If you got to ask, you ain't got it"[44]

9.1 Basics

If you are in a country with low online retail penetration, if you are an online pure-play anywhere, if you are not a premium trusted brand, or actually if you are just about anybody trying to sell through a non-store format, remember to reassure the customer. Many customers, even in very online literate markets, are still slightly dubious about it all. Lots of logos from organisations that specialise in trustworthiness are always worth the space (**Figure 23**):

Figure 23 - Reassuring German customers[45]

Clearly state policies, and make sure customers can find them. (I recently did a survey of top European sites, and it was surprising how often basic information like delivery prices and schedules were difficult to find). **Figure 24:**

Помощь	Help
Как сделать заказ	How to order
Доставка	Delivery
Оплата	Payment
Помощь	Help
Обратная связь	Feedback

Figure 24 - Basic Information Clearly Visible[46]

---

[44] Fats Waller explains what Jazz is
[45] From lidl.de
[46] From ozon.ru

Finally, make sure there is always a human available (*Figure 25* is from Apple China):

致电 400-666-8800
有疑问？尽管提问。周一至周五早八点至晚十点，或周六至周日早八点至晚八点，您可以打电话，向 Apple 专家咨询专业意见。

Figure 25 - US brand, Chinese helpline[47]

OK, these are all nice for any non-store channel, but what about multichannel? Refunds and Returns are a great place to start. The prospect of returning by post, and being confident of a refund, is intimidating for customers in any country. Only customer familiarity and a reputation for trustworthiness has made online fashion retailing, with its inevitably high returns rates, viable. It is noticeable in all countries that consumers have to become educated to purchasing online first, via simpler categories such as electronics, before they will take the risk of purchasing clothing online. For the brick-and-mortar retailer, reassuring customers that they can always return-to-store is an important differentiator against the pure-plays. Don't miss the chance to reinforce it (*Figure 26*):

Have a question about shopping at staples.com?

Can't find what you're looking for? Need to make a return?

Most Popular

How do I return an item?

Figure 26 - Returns, the top confidence issue[48]

---

[47] Apple's Chinese website
[48] Staples.com, US site, collage

9.2 Everything Else

For the true multichannel retailer, the way forward is not merely imagination plus technology. The critical concept is that the customer experience must be coherent and joined up. The customer must perceive that he/she is dealing with a single retailer, manifesting itself in different channels and formats, but still a single retailer. There must not be disconnects in the experience: to use a very simple example, store staff must know what to do when a customer who has ordered online wants to know why their order is late. It is this thinking which is behind two currently popular (and ugly) buzzwords – cross-channel and omni-channel. As usual in this field, there are many different definitions of the terms. The simplest way to think of them is that cross-channel retailing refers to joining up channels *after* checkout, omni-channel retailing to connecting channels *before* checkout.

Click-and-collect in store, is by this definition a cross-channel experience: the customer concludes checking out online, but then reverts to the store channel for delivery. Similarly endless aisles, where the customer orders in store but takes delivery at home are cross-channel.

Omni-channel, using the same definition, describes a customer purchasing experience which might include searching from a PC, reading reviews on a smartphone, getting recommendations from friends via Facebook on a tablet, adding to cart on smartphone, and placing an order at a kiosk in a store, tracking its progress on a tablet, and then writing a review on a PC again. See *Figure 7* for another example.

The terms are not as important as the underlying concept. In both cases, the key to a successful customer journey is that it must be seamless. If possible, each channel should know what the customer did on the previous channel. If this is technically impossible, then there should at least be no barriers. The future, which is only really starting to be developed in a fully multichannel way (as distinct from merely online), lies in personalising this experience – making it individually relevant to that customer. Personalisation is a topic of the later specific **Chapter 24**. However brick-and-mortar retailers should always remember that personal service, provided by a well-informed, service-focussed, human-being, is quite likely to be superior to most technology for the foreseeable future!

9.3 Top Takeaways

Cross-channel retail is the joining up of retail channels from checkout and afterwards.

Omni-channel retail is the joining up of the customer's experience up to and including checkout.

Customer experience across all phases and channels should be seamless and consistent.

Basic reassurance regarding security, payment options, and what to do when things go wrong is essential on non-store channels.

Refunds and returns are the number one reason why online customers seek help and reassurance.

An online pure-play should never be able to offer an overall experience superior to a fully multichannel retailer!

Chapter 10.   The Customer Experience

10.1   Connecting Personas and Differentiation

It has been my aim in the preceding chapters to suggest how a fully multichannel retailer can create a customer offer superior to either pure-play online or pure brick-and-mortar competitors. Each channel is deployed to advantage, and the customer is offered beneficial options for the completion of his/her shopping journey. The price to pay for these advantages is of course in complexity. Every channel is both specialism in itself and a part of a joined-up overall whole, and to be successful it is necessary to execute both specialisms and overall experience well.

There is some risk that continuously striving to develop new channels, new ways of shopping, new cross- and omni-channel customer journeys can become an end in itself, and not just a means to encouraging customers to choose to spend with you instead of a competitor. One of the many benefits of a well-founded personas/missions based approach to defining the customer experience is that it clearly prioritises what is important for your customers and therefore for your implementation, in a way that facilitates shared definition and understanding. To demonstrate the approach, the next sections work through an artificially constructed example in some detail. I am conscious that hypothetical and simplified examples are just that – simple and hypothetical, and lacking in the complex context that always exists in the real world. However, although a real case-study might have merits in terms of more sophisticated illustration of the ideas, an artificial example has the advantage of clarity.

10.2   Simplified Example

Back in section 3.3, we created a simplified customer persona and mission – in this case, me trying to buy chocolates for my wife's birthday from an overseas hotel room. I will briefly illustrate how to use them to help define the multichannel differentiation and requirements for a hypothetical speciality retailer of chocolates. In the interests of simpler grammar, I will call this hypothetical confectionary retailer ChoxBox. Let us assume that ChoxBox is a reasonably well-known name, with a brick-and-mortar outlet of some kind (either small store or some kind of franchise) on many high streets. Gift-giving is clearly a core customer mission for such a retailer, and let us further assume that ChoxBox has carried out basic research indicating that I (or rather my persona) is representative of a significant addressable customer segment i.e. my persona and mission are relevant and applicable to ChoxBox.

I will break down my customer experience step-by-step, illustrating how ChoxBox might set about winning my custom, drawing on the P.R.I.C.E framework.

10.2.1 Experience: Seamlessly omni-channel

In the first place, notice that I will almost certainly NOT start from a search engine, looking for search terms like "chocolate gifts" or something similar. I might use a search engine to find the address of ChoxBox's website, but I will then proceed directly there. ChoxBox is already a high street name I am familiar with. Therefore it has a big advantage over any online-only chocolate retailers. To a significant extent, my custom is there for ChoxBox to lose. Provided they meet my needs at every step, I should be given no reasons to step aside and look elsewhere. This is a cornerstone of omni-channel retail thinking.

10.2.2 Experience: Reassurance

When I arrive at ChoxBox's website, I want to be sure it *is* the same people as I am familiar with on the high street. I also want to be clear, since I intend giving not only my details but also my wife's details to them, that they will take an appropriate approach to her (our) data. I am NOT, at this step, so interested in products or offers. Although it sometimes feels like a waste of screen space to describe these experience basics, in the case of this defined mission it assuredly is not.

If ChoxBox cannot provide this reassurance, this could be a point where I start to look at a competitor – my omni-channel journey already has a potential break-point in it. Remember the One Second Rule!

10.2.3 Convenience

I am still not so interested in the products or offers. The next thing I need to know is whether I can get a gift to my wife specifically ON her birthday, which happens to fall on a Saturday. Therefore, still in experience basics, I need to be able to find this out quickly. If I have to start hunting through the website, or worse still, I can only find out *after* I have added a product to my cart and started to checkout, then I will quickly get diverted to checking out the competition.

There are at least a couple of ways for ChoxBox to meet this need. Firstly they could offer a nominated day premium delivery service (notice that this is NOT an Express service, where the product just comes as fast as possible; it is a designated day that I want to achieve). If this is the proposed, I want to know who the delivery service is... and if it is the British postal service, then I probably want some alternative options!

Alternatively, I could arrange for my wife to collect a parcel from a ChoxBox store near our house. Quite possibly the same postal service will still be delivering the parcel but: a) I don't know this, and in fact I have the perception that the order is picked in the store (even though this is probably not true); b) I have time to place the order in advance, and rely on the store to hold the parcel for a day or two waiting for my wife instead of only relying on the postal service to be timely. I also need some information at this point: the location of the nearest store.

Offering both options gives the choice to the customer; in a multichannel world, the customer is in charge, not the retailer. For the purposes of my illustrative example, we will assume that I'm going to choose the collect-in-store option.

10.2.4 Information: Inspiration

Note that according to my defined persona and mission, I am currently working abroad. On which channel have I been checking out these basics? Probably on my smartphone (which my persona says I will have) whilst sitting in a taxi stuck in traffic. Having validated the essentials, I'm going to wait until I can use a PC to look at possible products.

The website now needs to give me some ideas for gifts. I need options to browse thematically: "gifts for her", "gifts for occasions", "birthday ideas" etc. Note again that I'm not at home in the UK, where it is almost certain that I would have high speed broadband access. It's important that the website design takes a view on typical bandwidth available to customers. Even the term "broadband" means quite different things in different countries: from 128K in India, typically 2Mb+ in the UK for example.

10.2.5 Range + Information

My wife does not like honey or Turkish delight, but she is fond of coffee flavours. Our son is allergic to nuts. Notice that I have still not been tempted to break my customer journey and go to a competitor site. Missing nut allergy information is one reason why I might do so. My memory of the very small local franchise store is that the selection was extremely limited, and in fact when I last wanted to buy my wife a gift, I could not find a coffee flavours selection. I am here on the website on the assumption that a complete range will be offered, possibly with some options to exclude nuts and honey.

10.2.6 Price

At this point I *might* be tempted to check out a competitor price. But notice how committed I already am to this purchase. I have already researched delivery options, store locations, gift ideas, specific range information, allergy facts; I might even have used some sort of online tool to let me put individual chocolates into a box, write a personal message etc. A birthday gift for my wife is anyway not a price-sensitive purchase.

Assuming I am not tempted to start price-comparison shopping, I will now checkout. This is not the place to discuss website design in general, and checkout design in particular (I recently read an article entitled "87 ways to improve your website checkout"…). See **Chapter 21**.

10.2.7 Experience

I need to know the progress of this order. ChoxBox could send me emails, but emails are not my preferred option when am I overseas and with clients: I would much rather get an SMS, which I can pick-up immediately and act on instantly if there is an issue.

If there *is* indeed an issue, the SMS needs to tell me what to do – at the very least whom to call. Assuming all is well, it needs to tell me how to collect the gift at the store. In fact I am going to forward this SMS to my teenage daughter, and get her to take my wife to the store on her birthday morning as a surprise.

10.2.8 Convenience again

Therefore, the SMS needs to restate the store address and its opening times – I may remember this as the original purchaser, but I am not going to be the one making the collection.

10.2.9 Experience: Multichannel

The ChoxBox store staff must know what to do when my daughter shows them the SMS. There must be a sensible and simple way to verify the purchase and prove my wife's ID, despite the original purchaser (me) not being present. The staff must be immediately able to locate the right box, and there must be control processes to ensure that my wife does not receive someone else's gift by mistake.

ChoxBox now has new customers in its store, because their collect-in-store offer has caused me (existing customer) to bring my wife and daughter (potential new customers) there. Apart from hopefully delighting my wife with her gift, ChoxBox needs to do something to exploit this visit. Looking again at my persona, we remember that my wife is unenthusiastic about technology, but my daughter is fully wired. Coupons are an obvious repeat visit driver, but remember that they may well need to work online *and* in-store. A coupon to my daughter's smartphone could be an option.

10.3   Example Evaluation

We have now designed ChoxBox's preferred multichannel shopping experience for a particular relevant core mission – absentee-professional last-minute gift-giving. I just want to state again that the above example is necessarily both artificial and simplified. The next step should be to evaluate the resulting proposition, and understand whether or not we actually have created something sufficiently differentiated from the competition. In creating the persona and mission(s), we should already have established that this is a sufficiently large target to be worth addressing, preferably supported by data or at least by good experience-based knowledge. Will ChoxBox have a competitive advantage in this space if it implements the proposed customer journey, or is more needed?

P.R.I.C.E. provides one possible simplified framework, particularly adapted to multichannel retail, to evaluate this. To take this a step further, obviously we need to evaluate the competition, and as it seems just too artificial to create ChoxBox-2 to illustrate this. I will confine myself to outlining a possible extension to our framework, based on a weighted scorecard.

Step 1: we score the relative importance of each element of P.R.I.C.E. differentiation for this Persona performing this mission.

Step 2: we score the implementations of ChoxBox and its competitors.

Step 3: we evaluate the resulting weighted scores.

To work an example, I will use weightings on a 1=bad/unimportant to 5=good/important scale. Firstly we consider the relative importance of each element of P.R.I.C.E. for me and my mission:

Factor	Price	Range	Information	Convenience	Experience
Importance	2	3	4	5	4

Secondly, we score ChoxBox's implementation of this Mission by comparison with its competitors:

Factor	Price	Range	Information	Convenience	Experience
ChoxBox	1	2	3	5	4
Competitor A	3	4	2	3	2
Competitor B	4	4	3	3	3

As a way to illustrate the process, I have given ChoxBox a significant price and assortment disadvantage compared to its competitors.

Next, we multiply the importance by the scores, to derive weighted scores:

Weighted Scores	Price	Range	Information	Convenience	Experience
ChoxBox	2	6	12	25	16
Competitor A	6	12	8	15	8
Competitor B	8	12	12	15	12

Finally we total up for ChoxBox and its competitors. Usually the results are expressed as a percentage of the maximum possible total – in this case 5 * (importance of each factor) = 5 * (2 + 3 + 4 + 5 + 4) = 90:

Competitor	Total Score	% Score
ChoxBox	61	68%
Competitor A	49	54%
Competitor B	59	65%

I would have every sympathy with a client who expressed the view that this is a bit too much management consultancy and a bit too little reality! Nevertheless, it provides some underpinning to the intuitively reasonable idea that by excelling on factors important to the customer, in this case most especially convenience, it is possible to overcome a disadvantage in both range and price. In other real-world examples, this technique has helped drive the concept and decision-making; not usually because of the actual scores and percentages, but because the debate around the weightings and the scorings helps focus everybody on what is important and/or crystallises the debate around its key points. In general this is true of most "management consultant tools" of this type: the value is in structuring the process and debate, not in the actual outcome.

10.4   A real world example: Amazon versus Best Buy

Hypothetical examples don't come alive for everybody, so I'm going to briefly repeat the exercise for a currently high profile rivalry: consumer electronics at Amazon versus Best Buy. I don't intend providing long subjective assessments of their relative strengths and weaknesses in each aspect. Instead I'd suggest you score them yourself and draw your own conclusions. Of course you should use personas, but in this case I invite you to become the stereotypical representative customer, and score them yourself. Imagine you are planning to buy something, for example a good quality camera for your vacation.

First we need to weight the importance of the factors. Here are mine, what are yours?

Factor	Price	Range	Information	Convenience	Experience
Importance	5	4	5	3	2

Price is very important to me for an expensive product like a high-quality camera. I want a good selection to choose from. I don't know much about cameras so I need information and help. For once I haven't left it too late, so convenience is less important than it sometimes is.

Next we score each competitor on these factors. Here are my scores.

Factor	Price	Range	Information	Convenience	Experience
Amazon	5	5	2	3	3
Best Buy	3	3	4	4	3

I have the perception that Amazon is cheaper and carries a much wider range. However it's not the easiest place to starting looking if you don't understand the product in the first place and I'd probably rather be helped with my decision. There's a store up the road. (This last statement is not true, but for the purposes of this exercise, I'll assume it is true – there used to be one until they closed it!).

Now for the arithmetic bit, creating the weighted scores.

Weighted Scores	Price	Range	Information	Convenience	Experience
Amazon	25	20	10	9	6
Best Buy	15	12	20	12	6

And finally the results:

Competitor	Total Score	% Score
Amazon	70	74%
Best Buy	65	68%

On this extremely superficial analysis, Best Buy needs to change something. Improving my price perception would improve their score fastest. Closing my local store moves them from a close second to a distant second – not only will their convenience rating drop, but so will their experience score. The implications of this latter point will be considered in more depth in the chapter on stores - **Chapter 13**.

10.5   P.R.I.C.E. Summary

10.5.1 For the online pure-play

It is very difficult for an online pure-play retailer to be superior to multichannel competitors in <u>convenience</u>.

<u>Experience</u> can be equivalent, albeit in different ways. The disadvantage of not having personal service must be overcome.

<u>Range</u> (assortment) can be comparable.

<u>Information</u> can be comparable, but a parasitical approach to showrooming will be required (i.e. let your brick-and-mortar competitors be your showroom for customers who want to touch and feel the products). A strategy for mobile (see **Chapter 25**) may be required for this.

Online pure-plays probably have a lower cost-base, which should in turn enable a <u>price</u> advantage.

10.5.2 For the multichannel retailer

In many aspects of retailing a retailer with stores that embraces multichannel should have a superior customer offer compared to an online pure-play; in <u>information</u>, in <u>convenience</u>, in <u>experience</u>.

It should be possible to offer comparable range/assortment, which can be easier to sell to customers via Endless Aisles supported by face-to-face service.

Establish a strategy to address price.

If you are in a country where online pure-plays in your categories have not really succeeding yet in scaling up, but are simply scalping the lower end price points, then a sensible strategy is to stop them scaling up in the first place.

If this is not an option, use the advantages of having stores to join them and then beat them. Even in the most challenging markets in the world, 90% of all retail still takes place in store.

> We have shops, call centres and a website giving you flexibility in how and when you buy from us. The level of service we offer can't therefore be equalled by online or mail-order only retailers - and it's for this reason we don't match their prices. Examples include Dixons, Amazon or Play.com.

Figure 27 - A line in the sand[49]

10.6   Top Takeaways

The P.R.I.C.E. framework can be combined with the personas/missions approach to give structure to the process of defining differentiated multichannel customer journeys.

The same framework can be used to evaluate comparison with competitors.

Online pure-plays typically have a cost-base advantage over multichannel competitors, which can be translated into a price advantage.

Online pure-plays need to plan a showrooming strategy.

---

[49] John Lewis, price matching statement, 2012

Multichannel retailers hold most of the cards other than price when it comes to differentiation, and need to ensure they exploit these. If it is still possible, they should take steps to ensure pure-play competitors are stillborn. A strategy for addressing price is essential.

Part B – Fundamentals

Chapter 11.   Market Propensity

11.1   Country Propensity

11.1.1 Purchasing

Online retail purchasing requires broadband. Of course there are many other factors, but the key enabler for retail is high-speed access to the internet. Buying something online is a surprisingly complex, multi-step transaction, for which pictures are essential collateral. Yes, people without broadband will purchase online, but for it to take off in a country at scale, significant broadband penetration is the key necessary infrastructural development.

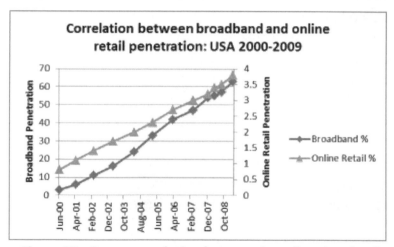

Figure 28 - Strong correlation between broadband and online retail[50]

Figure 28 is typical of the correlation in most countries. Before you object that the causality implied here is questionable - correlation does not imply causality – there is also a strong correlation between snapshots of broadband penetration and online retail penetration on a country-by-country basis. (The correlation is by no means perfect,

---

[50] Sources: www.census.gov , pew internet

many local demographic and cultural factors appeared to come into play, and genuinely like-for-like comparable broadband statistics from one country to the next are very difficult to obtain). What is more predictable is that as broadband rolls out, customer take-up of non-store retail will grow commensurately.

In countries with heavily urbanised populations and significant middle-classes, broadband rollout is typically a country-wide phenomenon. In developing or more rural countries, it can be very concentrated in particular locations or customer segments. For example in Russia, broadband penetration in Moscow and St Petersburg is estimated to be over 50%, but even in the relatively developed Central region, it is still well under 10%.[51] It is important, therefore, to consider not general country-wide statistics, but data relevant to your particular customer/persona demographics.

It is expected, although the case is at best partially proven thus far, that in countries where broadband will be delivered via 3G/4G mobile rather than by fixed line telecoms, a similar trend will be observed, but that because retail conversion on mobile is so much more challenging, the growth curve is likely to be much less steep. These countries typically also lack other enablers, such as reliable delivery services or credit-card penetration, which in turn slows down the transition to online.

We'll look in more detail at payment and internationalisation issues in separate chapters (**Chapter 20** and **Chapter 14** respectively), but payment methods are worth a brief diversion here. Note that even in Japan, with one of the highest penetrations of payment cards in the world (6.2 per adult), 18% of online transactions are still cash-on-delivery[52]. In Russia, still very much a developing online market, the percentage of cash-on-delivery rises to 64%[53]. It is easy for retailers familiar with sites that offer the standard Visa and Mastercard, Credit and Debit card options to forget that these are not the preferred

---

[51] Source: ertelecom
[52] Innopay, online payments 2012 report
[53] FOM, 2011

methods for customers across much of the globe. Credit card ownership is by no means a pre-requisite for online retailing.

And although lack of suitable parcel-delivery infrastructure in a country is indeed an obstacle to "traditional" e-commerce, it is worth remembering how much customers really do like click-and-collect (see **Chapter 26**) – typical take-up is 30-40% of all online transactions for a multichannel retailer with appropriate geographical coverage, even in countries with excellent logistics providers for parcel delivery. In countries with poor last-mile delivery services, this is an obvious opportunity for multichannel retailers to beat online pure-plays to the starting line.

11.1.2 Non-purchasing

It is, however, important to remember that multichannel retail does not mean that the *purchase* takes place online. It is much more likely that the research phase of the purchase takes place online than the actual checkout.

A concrete illustration is provided by India. The penetration of online retailing for purchase in India is extremely low, much less than 1% overall. Yet around 10% of Indians routinely access the internet, and two thirds of these use it to research purchases[54]. This 10% are of course generally more affluent and educated customers with much higher than average buying power. A wise Indian retailer will want to address these multichannel customers via online channels, even if that same retailer does not implement transactional online commerce.

At the other extreme over 80% of Americans researched significant purchases online before buying during 2011, but eCommerce purchase penetration in America, even of items which could specifically be considered "significant purchases" is nowhere near 80%.

11.2   Category Propensity

There are lies, damned lies, statistics and figures for online sales penetration. Although there are plenty of data points, defining an

---

[54] Nielsen wire, May 2011

"online" sale is increasingly difficult − if I order in-store from an endless aisle range and then have it delivered to my house, is that an online sale? It's certainly a multichannel sale. Through the haze of statistics, it is possible to discern a few general rules. Firstly, in some categories, logistics issues mean that multichannel models do not really work. I am not aware of a successful multichannel retail of either smoke or mirrors, for example. (See later chapter **Chapter 20**). A multichannel petrol/gas station or ice-vendor is unlikely to succeed.

Secondly at the other extreme, the absence of logistical challenges in selling music via digital download means that digital music downloads accounted for 32% of *global* record company revenues in 2011,[55] - and by implication, a much higher percentage in very online countries. (Just as another illustration of confusing statistics, over 50% of Dominos Pizza orders in the UK were apparently made online in 2011 − but a read of the small print reveals that this is only *delivered* orders.)

Thirdly, any retail model heavily dependent on either mail or telephone ordering has seen, in developed markets, a massive switch over to online. However, you could argue that mail/phone ordering is multichannel in the first place, and therefore that the change is just one of technology and not business model!

Fourthly, in countries such as China, C2C dominates the online space, representing over 70% of transactions in 2011[56]. Of course it is difficult to define whether a small trader on a marketplace such as TaoBao is actually B2C or C2C.

Fifthly, "traditional" business models which are challenging to translate into multichannel are, unsurprisingly, slow to migrate. The whole customer education cycle simply takes longer, and in some cases needs older customers to retire and be replaced by a new generation more comfortable with online purchasing. This can be seen, for example, in sectors in which traditional customers *expect* non-transparent pricing, and where the personal service element is

---

[55] International Federation of the Phonographic Industry
[56] People's Daily, 20th Feb 2012

very strong – building supplies for example. UK online DIY is an interesting case-study for a sector where an alternative business model (represented most obviously by Screwfix and Toolstation) has been developed to serve new customers in a new multichannel way, not so much changing as bypassing the traditional business model.

An interesting corollary is that once a new model does become established, customer take-up is often very rapid. Online grocery in the UK has been around for 15 years now, and is well established. Translating into cash & carry food retailing was slow to take-off, but the take-off has been spectacular when it eventually happened. Online transactions still represent only around 3-4% of UK food, but represent 16% of the food cash & carry market leader's sales[57], with all growth coming since 2006. However, even this story conceals some nuance. Although UK online grocery is only 4% of the market, online grocery is impossible economically (due to the cost of logistics) for cart sizes less than around €100. If all smaller carts are excluded, then online represents around 15-20% of all transactions, growing steadily. (See the chapter on online grocery - **Chapter 28**).

Finally, at the risk of a thousand-and-one counter-examples, I will propose a few guidelines to use as a baseline for very long-term planning, on the assumption that the products are not impossible to deliver, physical not digital, and generally "standard", whatever that means:

1. Assume an eventual high-watermark of around 25% sales to be non-store sales

2. Assume an eventual high-watermark of a *further* 25% of sales to be multichannel in some other way

3. There will be a phasing in most countries from "simple" categories (e.g. consumer electronics) through to categories requiring customer education and minor changes (e.g. clothing, which requires confidence and enhanced returns policies) through to very traditional or difficult categories

---

[57] See Booker plc annual reports

How long a particular category takes to reach these levels in a particular country is impossible to predict!

11.3   Top Takeaways

Broadband penetration is the most important enabler of transactional online retail in any country or market. It should be considered relative to the target customer group, not as a countrywide percentage.

Where broadband is delivered primarily by 3G/4G mobile, multichannel participation in retail is expected to grow faster than actual purchasing.

Online retail in many countries is not dependent on payment cards.

Although lack of last-mile delivery infrastructure in a country will inhibit online pure-play retailing, multichannel retailers can take advantage of click-and-collect to gain first-mover advantage.

Non-purchasing multichannel participation is much higher than purchase penetration. Customers are online at the research stage, even if not at the purchase stage. Retailers should follow their customers online, even in countries without high online purchase penetration.

Category participation is significantly determined by the practicalities of delivering the products.

Mail-order is a business model that translates very easily into online.

C2C dominates B2C in less developed markets.

Traditional categories which rely heavily on face-to-face contact are slower to migrate. New business models may be required. Catch-up can be very rapid once the transition is finally made.

A (very!) tentative very long-term planning high watermark of 25% of sales online, 25% otherwise multichannel, might be used as a starting assumption in the absence of other evidence.

Chapter 12.   Channel Conflict

12.1   Retailer internal perspective

12.1.1 The issue

A general hazard facing any brick and mortar business which becomes multichannel is that of Channel Conflict. In the simplest case, the (brick-and-mortar) <u>stores perceive that the non-store channels are "stealing our sales and customers"</u>. Taken to extremes, the multichannel retailer can end up creating entities which compete instead of collaborating. As the trend towards true multichannel continues, this is unsustainable, and current best-practice is increasingly to integrate (see the chapter on multichannel organisational design - *Chapter 23*), but this is not something that can be made to happen overnight.

Of course it is best if multichannel is implemented with full support from all stakeholders. The reality is inevitably that in a brick-and-mortar retailer introducing new retailing approaches, there are different levels of commitment and buy-in. The simplest way to ensure harmony in the early days of multichannel operations is to align KPIs and incentives, most especially in ensuring that stores are key supporters of all multichannel initiatives, whether these directly benefit the stores or not. (Typical contentious issues include increased rates of returns-to-store driven by non-store orders, handling costs of click-and-collect, reduction in takings at the store even while overall sales are growing, channel-specific promotional prices drawing attention away from the store).

12.1.2 A whole business approach

Strictly speaking, specific methods to avoid channel conflict probably belong in the organisation chapters later in the book (*Chapter 22* and *Chapter 23*). However I decided to introduce what is partly an accounting technique just here to illustrate another key point: multichannel affects the whole organisation.

"If your multichannel strategy does not change the job description of every individual in the organisation, then you have the wrong multichannel strategy."

Back-office teams like HR and Finance just as much a part of multichannel as an obviously impacted area like marketing or I.T. New KPIs need setting and measuring, just as much as online orders need delivering.

12.1.3 Financial treatment options

The following basic accounting treatments are typical of new online operations added to existing brick-and-mortar retail operations.

Separate P&L: Both sales and costs associated with the non-store operations are captured into a separate financial structure. (Whether this needs to be a separate legal entity is normally determined mainly by esoteric tax considerations).

Lost in the wash: Non-store is not treated as separate at all. While this is theoretically ideal, in practice it represents a level of organisational maturity that very few multichannel retailers are yet ready for.

Virtual store: The sales are captured separately, as are the specialist costs (e.g. for fulfilment), but cost areas like category management are shared across the business. In practice this is a recipe for exacerbating channel conflict issues and I suggest it should be avoided.

Wooden dollars (recommended): Online costs are captured into distinct central (head-office) cost-centres. Online sales (and cost of sales, so therefore margin) are attributed to stores, sometimes depending on the extent to which stores have to participate in the selling, fulfilment and returns process.

12.1.4 Wooden dollars in practice

The principle is simple: *all sales are store sales*, no matter which channel they were actually transacted on. A basic implementation of this approach is as follows:

i) Each sale and cost-of-goods (and by implication margin) made to a non-store customer is <u>ALWAYS assigned to a store</u>. The algorithm for so doing depends on the retailer business model; if a "home-store" for the customer is available, that is used. An practical alternative is to use postal/zip code catchment areas

ii) The stores are allowed to count these sales/margin towards their KPIs

iii) Because stores are benefiting in this way, they are also expected to handle any returns from the non-store channels in a standard way, even if this means writing the occasional stock-loss into the store books. Because non-store sales usually generate a higher returns rate than brick-and-mortar, retailers with a big enough percentage of non-store sales (e.g. in fashion) will adjust their store stock-loss KPI.

iv) All non-margin related non-store costs are kept in central cost centres attributed to non-store activities

v) The non-store teams get a normal P/L or KPIs, except that the sales & margin lines are "virtual" (thereby ensuring no double-counting). Sales, cost-of-goods (& margin) are written into this P/L so that the non-store team can be given business KPIs as though the eCommerce was a standalone business

A reasonable variation which is also sometimes seen is to pay stores a "commission" for handling non-store sales. This is especially common where click-and-collect type propositions exist, and stores therefore have a cost of handling associated parcels and customers. As customer journeys get more complex, and concepts such as endless aisle are implemented, commission-type arrangements run the risk of becoming impractically complex – the basic rule that all sales are stores sales rule is much easier to manage and, equally importantly, to explain to staff.

12.2 Supplier relationship perspective & D2C

12.2.1 D2C – direct-to-consumer

A temptation which manufacturers may not always resist is that of selling direct to the end-consumer. Online retail makes it not too difficult to do, and there are many potential advantages for the manufacturer: high margins, the opportunity for direct feedback to the customer, the chance to try new products at low risk. Customers who visit manufacturer websites are particularly good prospects: 75% of high-purchase propensity customers visited a brand website as part of their research, and 32% of those who did so actually purchased within a few days, according to one study.[58]

As a retailer, you might take the view that these efforts would be better directed. The manufacturer website might be a good information reference source for customers; it always has the imprimatur of authority. But if they can produce such good reference data on their site, why can't they make it available to you in an easily consumed format? Anything that helps reduce the product data management challenge (see *Chapter 15*) is worthwhile. New product trials can simply become part of your long tail / endless aisle. The manufacturer just needs to reduce the stock-risk in some way (see *Chapter 20*). And that customer feedback is from *your* customers.

12.2.2 Supporting *your* new channels

Rather than competing for your customers, there are some specific things that suppliers can do to help you with your multichannel retail activities:

Ready-to-use product data: managing product data is a nasty job. Suppliers need to make it easy for retailers to import it, already

---

[58] Channel Intelligence, 2010

clean, accurate, properly quality controlled and structured in an easy to consume format (preferably well-structured XML).

Ready-to-use merchandising data: the manual maintenance of cross-sells, up-sells etc is another time-consuming job. A ready-to-go dataset should be available as a starting point. It gives the supplier the advantage of discouraging cross-sells over to another supplier's products.

Unique products: price transparency is a huge issue in a multichannel world. Suppliers with larger customers who represent a significant percentage of their turnover should give consideration to providing them with variations on standard products that offer an escape from brutal price comparison.

Drop-ship the long tail: see *Chapter 20*. Ideally retailers would like to offer endless aisles without stock-risk, to improve their range credibility. There are various contributions suppliers can make, especially in the management of the long-tail.

Ready-to-ship packaging: see *Chapter 20*. Repackaging goods in an FC for online orders is expensive. Modify packaging so that it is suitable both for in-store logistics and customer-order shipping.

Simplify promotional structures: see *Chapter 21.* Complicated promotions like multisaves and linksaves are much more difficult to implement online than in brick-and-mortar.

Support the customer in the research phase: being the reference source (but in an agreed collaborative way that competes, not conflicts with the investment you may be making), and being responsive on social media channels that you cannot access.

12.3   Top Takeaways

Internal channel conflict is a significant risk to retailer adding new channels to their operations.

KPIs and performance measurements should be aligned to reward inter-channel collaboration, not competition.

Multichannel affects the *whole* organisation. If your multichannel strategy does not change the job description of everybody in the organisation, you have the wrong multichannel strategy.

All sales should be considered store sales.

The Wooden Dollars approach is recommended as a starting point; measuring the success of new channels while simultaneously distributing its benefits to existing ones.

D2C (direct to consumer) might be tolerated to support customer research; it should definitely be discouraged as a sales channel, product trial channel, or feedback channel.

Suppliers can contribute to supporting multichannel retail in various ways: ready-to-use product and merchandising data, unique products, managing the long-tail, ready-to-ship packaging, simpler promotional structures, a collaborative approach to online customer research.

Chapter 13.   Stores

13.1   Why so much space?

Some recent data from Germany:

1. Retail sales have essentially been flat overall from 2007-2012[59] (at around €440 Billion).

2. Online sales have grown at a compound rate of 16.6% annually in the same period, reaching 9% of all retail in 2011[60] (a growth of around €20 Billion)

3. Mail-order catalogue sales have reduced by around 25% over the same period (a reduction of approximately €4 Billion).[61]

In effect, brick-and-mortar store sales have declined by approximately 3.6% in that time. All the indicators are that online will continue to grow steadily in Germany – forecasts are typically in the 15% to 25% range. No analyst seems keen to predict that retail growth overall will be strong, and certainly not in the 20% range! The conclusion seems to be obvious: German retailers have too much brick-and-mortar retail space, and could be expected to begin to either downsize or close some stores.

It isn't noticeably happening yet, but then it didn't happen straightaway in markets "ahead" of Germany in terms of online retailing, such as the US or the UK. Of course some of the overall reduction in store space has come from retailers who failed to adapt at all to the multichannel world releasing a lot of space by simply going out of business, such as Schlecker. (UK examples include Woolworths, Zavvi and at the time of writing, Comet). Another tranche has come from retailers simply withdrawing from brick-and-mortar altogether as part of genuinely adapting to the new world (UK examples again include Dixons and Littlewoods).

---

[59] Tradingeconomics.com
[60] Federal bureau of statistics
[61] GfK, 2011

However one of the most obvious UK/US trends of 2012 is large retailers announcing changes in their space strategies to reflect the effects of multichannel. The biggest headlines, have of course gone to the biggest retailers. Best Buy announced the closure of 50 big-box stores in the US (as well as giving up on the lethal UK market altogether). Tesco's CEO announced that "we've called time on the old retail 'space race'"[62]. Overall the effect is strong enough for the majority of analysts to predict an ongoing reduction in store rental space costs, as demand for space continues to fall, and to identify this as being due more to new retail models than to the ongoing recession[63]. While this is bad news for landlords, it is extremely good news for multichannel retailers who will see an improvement in a key cost disadvantage compared to the online pure-plays.

Does this then imply that a retailer planning its multichannel strategy should plan for a reduction in overall store numbers?

13.2   Why so few?

What is especially interesting is that neither Best Buy nor Tesco plan to reduce store *numbers*. Best Buy intends opening 100 small format "mobile" stores alongside those 50 big box closures. Tesco intends to continue to roll out its smaller store formats in the UK, continuing to reduce the average journey-time for customers to a Tesco location of some sort, just not necessarily a hypermarket.

A clear illustration of why this might be so can be found in the published data from one of the most multichannel of all retailers, Argos (*Figure 29*).

---

[62] Philip Clarke, Tesco CEO: speech to world retail congress, September 2012
[63] See for example ING "the more clicks, the less bricks", October 2011

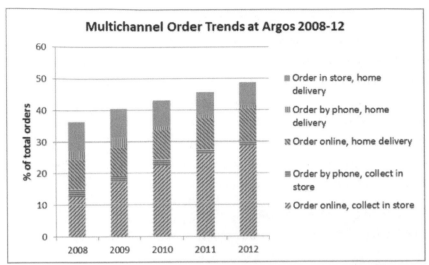

Figure 29 - customer Multichannel trends at Argos[64]

One story is not unexpected, and consistent with the data from Germany cited above: telephone orders have continued to reduce steadily in importance, in the same way that German data shows a steady decline in traditional mail-order (which includes telephone ordering). Much more interesting, and far less predictable, is that the percentage of internet orders for home delivery has remained rather static for the last few years. In part this reflects mix (these orders are often for large items such as beds or white goods), but it sits in stark contrast with the relentless growth in order-online-collect-in-store (or Check & Reserve, as Argos calls it – the difference being that as a customer you don't pay online, you pay in the store when you pick up your goods).

So have brick-and-mortar store sales fallen as a proportion at Argos? Well, yes, initially as internet retailing was adopted by UK consumers, a percentage of the in-store business switched to internet home delivery, paralleling the ongoing switch from telephone/mail-order to internet ordering. But in the published data, certainly for the last 5 years, the *percentage of sales that use the brick-and-mortar*

---

[64] Home Retail Group Annual Report 2011/12

store channel in some way or other has remained rather static, but the way in which customers use the stores has changed.

One way in which it has changed is the continuous increase in the use of click-and-collect (or the instantaneous step-change in take-up in any retailer that introduces it). Does this mean more stores are required; why not use services such as Kiala or Relais Colis, which allow the customer to choose from an extremely convenient local pick-up point? The answer lies in some very interesting recent quotes from some leaders in this space. For example:

"35% of our orders are being collected in store, and even more than that from customers in a store catchment area. Of those we also know that a significant proportion are truly incremental, as customers would not have purchased from us without it. Add on the fact that 25% of people make an unplanned add on purchase when in the store…"[65]

Other retailers are starting to report similar figures regarding unplanned add-on purchases in the 20-40% range. The conclusion: click-and-collect can actually drive incremental extra sales in the collecting store. This is only going to work if there is a store within a reasonable drive-time. A sensible recommendation might be to offer a Relais Colis style service for areas beyond a reasonable store-catchment journey-time and use it to "fill in the gaps" in national coverage with a pure pick-up location unsupported by a true store. In compact countries, such as the UK or Netherlands, where 80-90% population coverage within reasonable journey time is relatively easy to achieve, click-and-collect alone is probably good enough. In other countries, the dual-channel approach might commend itself.

13.3   The Digital Store

The second way in which customers are using stores differently is in the area of "service". The most familiar example is probably Apple's stores (or unfamiliar: I remember my astonishment when the guy in

---

[65] Andy Fraser, Director of eCommerce at House of Fraser, interview October 2012 with eConsultancy

the Apple store asked me if I had an appointment – to handover my money to Apple...!). The traditional "pay here" desk behind which half the store staff stand in a rather static, and passively unhelpful, way is changing.

Increasing numbers of retailers are giving their staff a more roving role, supported by tablet computers. The tablet may provide many services, and might have a whole selection of features or dialogues, but at its most fundamental its purpose is to try and help ensure that the staff-member is at least as knowledgeable as the customer, and can actually add some value to the customer while he/she is in store. The added value, directly or indirectly, increases the chance of a sales conversion. And no, I don't have any trustworthy data points in support of that assertion – it's too new. There is plenty of anecdotal evidence, and it seems intuitively reasonable, particularly in retailers who employ large numbers of seasonal, peak-time or other temporary staff who inherently have little deep knowledge of their domain, and for whom a "wizard" in support can help them to step-change their ability to engage with the customer.

To supplement the staff with the tablet is an increasing array of digital experiences in store (and in some case carried over into the online experience too), from virtual fitting rooms to massive TVs to gift-registry kiosks to... you name it. Interestingly the retailer with the clearest perspective on all this is an online pure-play:

"[we are] competing for a percentage of our... customer's <u>time</u> as well as an increasing percentage of their... purse."[66] *[my underlining]*

Besides all this gadgetry and wizardry to tempt and dazzle the in-store customer, retailers are increasingly competing for a percentage of their customer's time in a more direct way. Giving up on futile attempts to stop customers using mobile devices to check out their competitors while in-store, savvy retailers have now decide that offering free wireless broadband in-store at least keeps the customer a) happy and b) in there. Rather as click-and-collect leads to incidental

---

[66] Asos.com, annual report 2011/12

purchases, simply extending visit times in a pleasant environment might lead to increased sales.

13.4   Mix

Finally, having re-sized your stores, reconfigured your store staff to make them more digital and service oriented, rearranged your stores to make them more of a leisure destination, redesigned your operating procedures and use of space to enable click-and-collect and endless aisle kiosks, you can reconsider your product assortment.

Developing the endless aisle concept, or even simply excluding "awkward" products from your store range, allows you to optimise your stores while still maintaining that critical Kompetenz discussed earlier. Some products are less than ideal in stores: pillows are a good example. They have a low price point, high space consumption (and logistics costs), and are unlikely to be a top-seller for most retailers. Nevertheless if you are operating in home-wares categories, you probably have to offer them. Some products are equally suboptimal in a non-store situation: mirrors and heating-oil are two examples.

Just to summarise, multichannel might change your stores in many ways: size, numbers, layout, concept, service, POS, processes, assortment mix. This is a particularly clear illustration of the difference between a multiple channel approach and a multichannel approach (see **Part D**). In genuine multichannel your stores are "just another channel", albeit by far the most important one, and are as much or as little impacted as all those new channels like web, mobile, social or even call-centre that might more immediately spring to mind under the banner of multichannel.

13.5   Top Takeaways

Retailers, especially big-box retailers, are considering reducing the average size of their stores. Overall demand for store space is expected to decline in more developed multichannel countries.

In parallel, the same retailers are increasing the overall number of their, as convenience/proximity to the customer becomes more important.

Click-and-collect, especially from stores near the customer, is a driver of incremental sales. Parcel collection services may be a poor substitute, useful in areas where you have no local store.

The in-store experience is becoming increasingly a digital experience. Technology is increasingly being used to help the in-store sales assistant offer better service to customers.

Multichannel offers options to optimise the assortment-mix in stores.

Chapter 14. International

14.1 Introduction

WWW stands for World Wide Web. In theory this represents an opportunity. Anybody with a website can reach any consumer on the globe who has internet access. International parcel delivery services like DHL or Fedex can usually reach most places. The world is your e-oyster.

Unfortunately the practical obstacles are usually rather formidable, and tend to be under-estimated. That's not to say they are impossible, especially between countries with linguistic and cultural affinities (the UK and Australia for example, or US and Canada), or where you might have a large expat community. And cross-border commerce represents a growing opportunity. It is estimated that 6% of US eCommerce was cross-border in 2009, but this is expected to become 15% in 2015, primarily branded apparel and related categories where there is a strong reason for the consumer to reach out overseas for specific items not available locally at reasonable prices.[67] As an illustrative example, Asos, the fashion brands online pure-play retailer based in the UK, made 59% of its sales overseas in 2012[68], up from 43% the previous year. Much like Amazon however, Asos is increasingly blurring the boundary between cross-border commerce from an essentially UK operation, and an international operation using local facilities in each country (including websites, logistics, local offices etc).

The tasks involved in setting up a totally new overseas operation are outside the scope of this book. However the more basic challenges of selling to overseas customers, possibly via a different "version" of your online presence are more accessible, and covered in the next section. Even this could be the subject of a whole book by itself, so I'm going to just touch on the surface of the basics.

---

[67] Source: Pitney Bowes, in turn citing Forrester
[68] Asos annual report 2011/12

14.2 Cross-border eCommerce

14.2.1 Language

Obvious isn't it?

The trouble is that some less obvious things are also language dependent. Foremost amongst these are SEO and SEM (see later **Chapter 18**), which are generally quite text / keyword specific activities, and for which straightforward translation simply doesn't work – there are too many cultural differences, idiomatic expressions, and language structure differences to make this just a question of repeating the same activities but via a translation service.

Secondly, you have probably invested a fair amount of effort in making sure your first language "fits" nicely onto any web pages or more especially mobile site. Words or phrases which are a different length will mess this up. Areas like site navigation, product hierarchies, and menus are particularly vulnerable. More extreme issues arise in adapting right-to-left languages like Arabic.

Thirdly any successful online retail site relies heavily on its internal search (see **Chapter 21**), and to work well this has to be "tuned", which is again a language idiosyncrasy dependent task and not a matter of straightforward translation. If you step outside of purely alphabetic languages, into e.g. Japanese or Chinese, then this is a huge challenge.

Fourthly your product master data (see **Chapter 15** and **Chapter 19**) may need duplicating. Once you have experienced the full horror of this task in one language, you may be less than enthusiastic about repeating it in another!

I don't want to attempt to get into regulatory issues around product labelling in any detail, but if you are operating for example cross-border inside the EU, you'll need to ensure you are linguistically as well as regulatory compliant.

Last but definitely not least, how will your customer service team handle queries and calls?

14.2.2 Preferred online channel

If you targeting another highly developed country, then it's possibly obvious that you should replicate your existing online channels. If you are targeting a country such as China or India, it's worth pausing first. The majority of internet access in these countries is via mobile. So the first thing to replicate might *not* be your existing website. See **Chapter 25**.

14.2.3 Payment Methods

You *cannot* assume that customers are ready and willing to pay by the standard methods accepted in your home country. As I type this, I have a study in front of me of the payment methods offered by the top online stores across just 9 major European countries. And there are 40(!) of them.

In some cases, the differences are just variations within a family – a local credit card scheme for example. You can choose to offer it, find suitable infrastructure, and proceed without too much difficulty. However in other cases, alternative payment methods affect the whole flow of orders, and potentially profitability and pricing – there is a huge difference between payment "up-front" via iDeal in the Netherlands and payment "on delivery" by old-fashioned cash in Russia. (Payment policy questions such as these are discussed in **Chapter 20**).

An obvious related question is whether you will try to offer local currency pricing.

14.2.4 Delivery / Shipping

A surprisingly frequent trivial omission is amending the checkout pages on websites to accept alternative address structures and international phone numbers (especially the non 0-9 characters '+' and '()' as in +44 (0) 1234 567890).

Duty thresholds vary enormously from country to country and so do customs issues. You can of course just make the customer responsible, but it won't encourage sales. Operating fulfilment locally is obviously a way around this, but inevitably that adds costs in both operations and stock, and is only worthwhile in markets which are big enough for you. Otherwise you might be limited to cross-border selling within customs unions such as the EU.

And a key confidence issue to persuade customers to buy online is Returns. Sellers of apparel to reasonably developed markets need to provide a local returns address. Elsewhere it is of course easy to overstate this need when selling into countries with a strong caveat emptor culture (India, for example). Whether your home country has a high consumer protection culture or a more caveat emptor approach, make sure you understand the local expectation in your target market.

Finally some products simply cannot legally be sold in this way across border in some countries. There are no general rules, you have to check case by case.

14.2.5 Cultural differences

Never ever underestimate these!

Before hunting for subtle differences of nuance, don't forget the "staring you in the face" issues. For example, if you sell apparel, then it is the Summer Season in Australia in December, and the Wet Season in India in July. (For northern hemisphere retailers, Australia is an excellent place for an end-of-season clearance store! Don't bother with a separate website, just run it on an eBay Gallery – see **Chapter 27**).

If you are just planning to make your goods available to overseas customers by simply offering international shipping and payment from an existing website, then cultural differences are probably not an issue. You are not investing much time and effort, and the rewards will be commensurate.

If you are seriously planning to target a second country, then my advice is very simple: go visit it in the company of a (native) resident before you do anything else. The first time I did a professional assignment in India some years ago, I was astonished at how many basic assumptions about how a business should operate needed to be reconsidered – the most frequently arising being my automatic assumption that anything labour-intensive needs to be automated. Remember that these assumptions work in reverse too.

14.3   Top Takeaways

Cross-border commerce, enabled by online, is a significant current growth area and opportunity.

Language differences are not just a matter of translating content. External search (SEM and SEO) and internal search may need re-implementing. Site layout may be impacted. Customer service needs to be multilingual.

If you target markets are developing countries, consider a separate mobile site.

Payment methods are different, and often quite specialised, in every country. Differences may significantly impact operations and order lifecycle (See *Chapter 20*), especially differences between pay-on-site and pay-on-delivery.

Local legal issues, product labelling, duties and customs must be addressed.

Logistics/shipping solutions need to consider Returns.

Don't actively target somewhere you've never visited!

Chapter 15.   Product Master Data

15.1   Introduction

This might seem a curious topic to include in a section entitled Fundamentals, but I firmly believe it belongs here. If you are already online, you will already be aware of how critical the topic is. If you are still planning to go online, then be warned: in every online implementation project I have ever seen or been involved with, product master data management always ends up being *the* critical path task for launch.

It isn't just for implementation either. Even the smallest step-change to the multichannel proposition you offer to your customers tends to involve yet another master data management (MDM) challenge. Adding click-and-collect? You need to flag all the eligible products. Adding cross-sells or recommendations? You need to manage all the connections or exclusions between products. Adding an endless aisle in a category? Probably thousands more products requiring MDM. New season range change? More MDM. Special festival period offer? Still more MDM. You get the picture.

There are two reasons for this. Firstly in any online retail proposition, unlike a brick-and-mortar store you are not selling a product. You are selling a <u>description</u> of a product, <u>plus a promise</u> to somehow get it to the customer. The description and associated things like pictures <u>IS</u> the product as far as the customer is concerned. It needs to be accurate, enticing, and well, descriptive.

Secondly, data also describes "how" your online offer will behave, and how the product will appear. A very simple example to cheer up this page full of otherwise rather bad news: where does this particular product sit in the browsing hierarchy? Is it a 'red -> wine', or a 'wine -> red'? Somewhere, this decision and information has to be entered as an item of data. Strictly, this "how" data is not *master* data, it is *merchandising* data. For many practical purposes, the distinction is irrelevant because in all except the very largest and most complex organisations with the most sophisticated IT systems, the same people using the same systems end up doing the work. (We'll return to this topic in the IT section later **Chapter 21**. As with all things IT and multichannel, inevitably it somehow isn't quite as simple as I've painted it in this introduction).

In other words, master data defines *what* you are selling and the closely related concept of merchandising data defines *how* you are selling it, which is pretty fundamental to any retail business. The standard baseline planning benchmark is that it takes 25 FTE minutes per SKU to set-up or maintain the necessary master data. Or put another way, 1 FTE can manage 4000 SKUs per year. One of my clients had 800,000 SKUs...

The cost benefit case can be quite challenging. One take on this, as discussed in more depth already in **Chapter 7**, is to take a hard look at exactly how much data you need to capture – do you really need to become *the* reference source for this information online – and use that approach to reduce the costs. The alternative, of course, is to increase the benefits, and adapt a truly multichannel approach to the exploitation of master data.

15.2   Master Data and Multichannel

The beauty of high quality master data is that it can enhance <u>all</u> your channels. Arming a store sales assistant with good quality, easily accessible reference data can step-change the experience they give your customers and step-change their conversion rate with it. Concepts which would not previously have been possible, such as in-store service kiosks (which should be manned: unmanned kiosks do not work) or a portable equivalent delivered via tablet, become possible.

Most call-centres know that their stellar agents are often the ones with the best understanding of the product catalogue. It now becomes possible to bring other agents up to a least a comparable level, although stars still tend to remain stars of course. Similarly, unpleasant costs such as high returns-rates can be reduced by ensuring that call-centres, and also customer-service desks in store, have access to essential information about the product.

Fancy one of those very sexy "retail walls" such as Tesco are operating in South Korea or a portable cube like Delhaize in Belgium (*Figure 30*), design to be scanned by mobile phone? Master data is the foundation for such concepts too, whose business cases go well beyond just their pure sales value in terms of incidental advertising benefit.

Figure 30 - Delhaize Mobile Cube

Anecdotally, many head-office functions also benefit from the ready accessibility of product reference information, although it is difficult to quantify this in a business case. (Some retailers have experimented by going further and make (some of) their data available to 3rd parties to develop applications that in turn, drive sales for the retailer (see affiliates later in *Chapter 18*). At best this has rather mixed success.)

The next logical step is to enhance this basic data with rather less easily captured "knowledge". There are already some tools on the market which begin to attempt to interact with online customers in the way that a (human) sales assistant would, for example by asking a series of questions that attempt to drill down to the customer's need. These are essentially "knowledge based" and/or even self-learn dynamically (operating in a manner not dissimilar to the child's game animal, vegetable or mineral). Human beings remain a much better solution than IT for the true multichannel retailer, but even people still benefit from additional prompting, guidance and tools. Knowledge management systems are relatively well established – they are just better organised memories really – but screen-based conversational/interactive sales is still in its infancy, and any business case is likely to be speculative.

Sales channels with data as their basis need to be heavily specified by additional merchandising data, including up-sells, cross-sells, product hierarchies (see taxonomy later in *Chapter 19*). Sales channels operated by people need to equip their operators with tools to leverage the knowledge in an efficient way. *Figure 31* illustrates the flow.

Figure 31 – Master Data & Knowledge Flow

Business cases for master data in data channels are probably most easily made on the basis of measures such as increased cart-size. Business cases for human channels most easily made on the basis of increased conversion or reduced costs (in various ways, from the straightforward e.g. reduced returns rates, to the more challenging reduced labour costs – cheaper people with better tools can replace better people with poor tools).

Master data is *the* fundamental building block of multichannel retail. It should not be treated as an incidental nuisance. Master data management is at least as important a discipline as logistics when it comes to the success of your strategy (indeed I shall argue in the chapter on organisation - *Chapter 22* - that it is on a par with logistics in many ways). If you are new to online retailing, put it on the critical path for your implementation project, and do not underestimate the resourcing required to manage it. What looks like a simple clerical task is actually a highly skilled job, upon which the success of your entire implementation and strategy will depend. More on this topic in *Chapter 19*.

15.3   Top Takeaways

Product master data is the foundation of multichannel retailing.

If it is a new discipline for your retailer, put it on the project critical path and start now!

An online retail channel is not selling products, it is selling descriptions of products (plus a delivery promise). The descriptions are therefore critical.

Master data describes the products (the *what*) you are selling. Merchandising data describes *how* you sell them. For smaller retailers, or with less complex IT systems, the distinction may be theoretical rather than practical.

Master data can improve more than just online channels. The effectiveness of store and call-centre staff can be enhanced by good data, which can be further enhanced by knowledge management solutions.

The planning benchmark assumption is that good quality master data requires 25 minutes per SKU to source and capture. 4000 SKUs therefore require approximately 1 man-year to set up.

Much more detail on the topic of master data is in Chapter 19.

Chapter 16.   Available to Promise

16.1   Definition

As stated in the introduction to **Chapter 15,** in any online retail proposition you are selling a <u>description</u> of a product, <u>plus a promise</u> to somehow get the described product to the customer. That chapter discussed the description, this chapter discusses the promise. The promise actually consists of two parts:

A shipping promise. This is straightforward, and might include various options for the customer such as express delivery, pick-up-in-store, nominated time etc. I'll discuss these further in the chapter covering delivery (**Chapter 20**);

A stock promise: when will the items be available to start shipping to the customer?

Available-to-Promise (ATP) is usually considered to refer to the second point. ATP is actually a bit of IT jargon, but the concept is so fundamental to multichannel retail that it deserves better in life than relegation to an IT three letter acronym (TLA...).

16.2   Implementation

For many people ATP's most familiar manifestation is seen on Amazon's website (see **Figure 32**), with its statements such as "usually despatched within 5 to 10 days".

£14.50 Paperback

Usually dispatched within 4 to 6 weeks

£18.98 **£18.24** Hardcover

Only 2 left in stock - order soon.

£12.99 **£11.69** Paperback

In stock but may require up to 2 additional days to deliver

Figure 32 - Availability Promises[69]

Notice how this promise varies from the very specific "2 left in stock" to the rather vague "usually dispatched within 4 to 6 weeks", which really doesn't commit to anything except an expectation that it will turn up eventually but you might be waiting a long time. This spectrum from specific to vague reflects Amazon's control over the stock and the processes. One might reasonably infer that the two left in stock are in an Amazon warehouse, whereas the four to six week item has to be purchased from a secondary supplier (and in the case I used to make the collage, actually from overseas).

There are some important refinements of this that are particularly relevant to multichannel retailers. Specific promises can only be made when you have tight control over stock and processes. How many retailers really have firm control over their in-store stock? You may well have good processes at start and end of day, but what about intraday, when (hopefully) your stores are full of customers with items in their shopping baskets which are neither on your shelves – and therefore available – nor rung through your POS – and therefore unavailable. In-basket stock is in a kind of limbo for the purposes of availability promises. This is especially important if you are operating some sort of click-and-collect proposition where the items are pre-picked in store (see **Chapter 26**).

Similarly if you operate, as many multichannel retailers do, a supply chain where the Fulfilment Centre for eCommerce receives its stock from the same source(s) as your stores, can you realistically make any

---

[69] Collage from Amazon.co.uk, November 2012

commitment to the level of stock deliveries into that Fulfilment Centre tomorrow? There are a number of reasons why this might not be the case. For example:

Uncertain supply: you can't guarantee the precise timing and volumes which will be delivered by your suppliers;

High efficiency: you currently have very efficient logistics, with strong "one touch" processes operating, but where breakages, non-conformance and similar issues which affect saleability are therefore only discovered at the last possible moment;

Channel conflict: you prefer not to prioritise allocations of stock to eCommerce over allocations to stores in the event of any shortage;

Unpredictable velocity: you have items whose rate of sale is hard to predict. Typically this applies especially to the long tail.

In a brick-and-mortar store environment, none of this precision matters quite as much. The item is either on the shelf when the customer tries to pick it up or it isn't. Availability is of course important, and you will disappoint customers if items are missing, but there is no complicated promise for the future. Shelf availability is an instantaneous fact. In an online environment, by contrast, the item is not picked immediately the customer puts it into their cart. It is probably not picked immediately the customer checks-out either. Availability on the shelf or pick-face is an accumulation of results of complex business processes spread over an extended time period.

ATP is also probably the most complex area of your IT, for the simple reason that it lies on the interface between multiple systems – maybe at least website, stores, logistics, shipping, order management, and probably others. In almost all IT ecosystems and projects, the "difficult" bit is interfacing *between* component systems, not the implementation of the self-contained components themselves. Having a critical business process spread across boundaries in this way intrinsically adds complexity.

So in ATP lies an inherent conflict. You want to make the best possible promise to your customers, maximising both availability itself and also optimising the promise as part of competing on convenience. Making best possible promises means diving headlong into some of the most complex business processes and IT systems in your business. Complex processes are risky processes. Disappointing customers who believe they have successfully checked-out and a just waiting for their goods to be delivered is extremely bad, much worse than not having an item available on a brick-and-mortar store shelf. Very likely such a customer will need a lot of convincing to return to you and try again.

For the retailer new to multichannel, the best advice is to keep it simple. Only promise what you are 100% certain you can deliver, even at the apparent risk of missing sales opportunities. Experience says that the cost of any sales lost in this way will be far lower than the cost of disappointing large numbers of your most loyal customers. The realisation of such a policy clearly depends on how you set up your fulfilment, but the simplest case is that of a dedicated stock location, and a policy that says you will only promise to customers stock which is definitely in that stock location in a fit condition for sale, and which has not already been sold to another customer.

For the multichannel retailer scaling up, these and related issues (see Order Lifecycle, **Chapter 20**) lie behind the justification for major investments in the implementation of sophisticated order-management engines, often running to into millions (in any currency!) of costs.

16.3   Not available to promise

This issue really doesn't merit the headline "Fundamentals" which this section of this book is supposed to be about, but invariably comes up in any discussion of the topic so I've included it here: what should an online channel (usually the website) display when a particular SKU is theoretically included in the range but is temporarily out of stock?

Back-orders are notoriously challenging to handle, especially if your IT back-office systems are not yet very sophisticated. Therefore the choice often boils down to either display it but tell the customer they cannot add it to their cart, or don't display it at all. Displaying it unavailable risks disappointment, not displaying it damages your marketing (especially SEO marketing).

The recommended answer, assuming you don't feel confident to handle back-orders (and I strongly recommend that you don't unless you are *very* confident of the back-office system provision – don't improvise it), is to consider the issue at a category or sub-category level. A category with say 5% of its items out of stock actually looks fine, and anecdotally is actually a positive statement to customers: we are in control of our stock, our promises are real, there are sufficient sales on this website to cause out-of-stock situations to occur. A category with 50% of its items unavailable just looks pathetic and tells the customer to try a competitor instead: don't display the unavailable items in such a category.

16.4   Top Takeaways

An online retail channel is not selling products, it is selling descriptions of products plus a delivery promise. The promise is made up of a shipping promise and a stock promise. Available to Promise (ATP) usually refers to the latter.

Stock promises made about in-store stock are especially challenging.

Channel conflict can impact multichannel retail ATP.

ATP is relatively more critical for online channels than general stock availability is for brick-and-mortar channels.

ATP can become very complex: it typically lies at the nexus of many of your systems and processes. Keeping it simple is important to start with; once you want to go beyond simple, expect to need to make a significant investment in systems.

Low frequency out-of-stocks may add credibility to a category online; high frequency out-of-stocks reduce it.

Part C – Basics

At its core, Part C is a "how to go online" guide for the retailer who is not yet online. There are two target audiences, but the first is probably the primary one:

i) Existing brick-and-mortar retailers who are considering adding a serious eCommerce channel to their existing store channel. This is a multichannel retail handbook. Brick-and-mortar retailers planning to add new transactional channels are therefore one of its primary target audiences. This section generally approaches issues from the perspective of a retailer wishing to make this step from mono-channel to multichannel.

ii) A potential start-up online pure-play. However this book cannot be a guide to "how to become a retailer". Topics such as "How to Buy" are definitely out of scope. I assume you have all such basic retail competencies in place or available, and look only at the variations and additions that are implied by taking them online

Part C is not intended to be read standalone; it assumes you are aware of the contents Part A and Part B. It is structured to reflect the business case you will need to build, considering firstly estimating the sales opportunity, and then looking at the key cost areas in turn.

Chapter 17.   Forecasting Sales

17.1   Cannibalisation

Any new channel will cannibalise an existing one. A new eCommerce channel will, therefore, cannibalise sales from your stores. It is extremely difficult to measure this effect, and so the usual rule of thumb applied is that around 50% of any "new" sales will in fact not be incremental overall. The few data points available tend to suggest that this might be rather pessimistic, but to a significant extent it depends heavily on whether your competitors are already online as well.

Before you halve the benefits line in your business case, and then disgustedly decide it isn't actually worth it at all, it is worth returning to some basics.

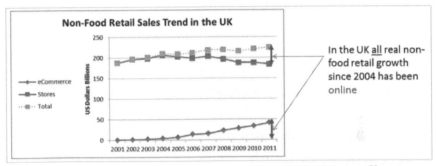

Figure 33 - Non-Food Retail Growth Trend in UK[70]

Figure 33 illustrates a critical point: eCommerce does NOT create new money in customer's wallets. New channels are competing for wallet-share with existing channels. You may recall from Chapter 1 that your best customers will be expecting you to be on multiple channels, a proportion which will grow as adoption of new channels grows in your market. If you aren't on these new channels, they may well switch to a competitor who is. This leads to a key point:

If you don't cannibalise your brick-and-mortar stores yourself, then somebody else will cannibalise them instead.

---

[70] Data from UK Office of National Statistics & British Retail Consortium

It is very important to separate this statement into its two different consequences. Firstly, your eCommerce business case should claim <u>all</u> its forecast sales, not just the truly incremental part. Secondly a completely different business case should consider the consequences to your stores of potentially reduced sales (see **Chapter 13**).

17.2 Competitive Landscape

In order to effectively model the sales opportunity, it is helpful to consider the key states in which an online market might be, in your countries/categories. The three basic situations are: 1) Highly developed online; 2) undeveloped online; 3) fragmented. A simple template is provided for each in turn. I have created example high level assessments for illustration. *Please be aware that I have made up the data and examples for illustration only.*

17.2.1 Highly developed online market

...but not including you!

The size of the potential eCommerce market can usually be determined from publicly available data, and competitors are usually well known. The general growth of eCommerce is also usually well tracked and projected out in various publicly available studies. Suggested assessment template with example:

Market: UK B2C Wine

Market Size: around GBP 500M

Growth: approximately 11% per year

General landscape: a very developed market, dominated by three large players. There are also numerous specialist and non-specialist "wine-clubs", especially those run by the Sunday newspapers or offered as rewards by the major points-based loyalty schemes. Many of these are in fact fulfilled by the big three.

Key competitor #1: AAAA.com, 40% share. Differentiated by Range and Experience. *Range*: deep-range online pure-play. Subscription models drive a significant proportion of revenues. *Experience*: celebrity wine-writers add cachet to the site.

Key competitor #2: BBBB.com operated by a leading supermarket, 15% share. Narrow core range with approximately 2000 SKUs. Differentiated by Convenience, Experience and Information. *Convenience*: leverages online grocery delivery vans to offer precisely timed delivery slots. *Experience*: exclusive club feel. Multichannel strongly leveraged, with store-based events branded as club-exclusives, and promotional calendars synchronised offline and online. *Information*: magazine and associated secondary club brand.

The focus when considering how to model sales (see below) will be on how your differentiation will allow you to capture some market share from these established competitors. Your differentiation approach will need to be very strong.

17.2.2 Undeveloped Online Market

In such a market the focus will be on understanding the category offline market, and then extrapolate by understanding general online trends. It is also necessary in such a market to examine whether basic hygiene factors for online retailing such as broadband, banks offering secure online payment connections, or last-mile delivery exist. In some markets (India is a good example) these are "just happening" and a first mover opportunity may well exist. Secondary evidence is available from information on non B2C online commerce such as eBay for example. See the topic Market Propensity (**Chapter 11)** for further information. Suggest assessment template with example:

Market: India, Jewellery

Total market size: Approximately 65000 crore Rs

Online market size: 80 crore Rs, approximately 0.1% of all sales

General landscape: Highly fragmented market. Approx 6% of market taken by large players such as YYYY (4%). Some single-state chains. Otherwise all local players. However an item of jewellery sells on eBay in India every 6 seconds, according to the latest figures.

General online retail landscape: Retail eCommerce as a whole is forecast to grow by at least 30% year on year, over and above underlying retail growth of 15% year on year.

Constraints: Delivery. Last mile delivery, especially of high value items, is available only in large cities. Cross state-border taxation issues remain a concern.

Constraints: Payment. Payment infrastructure is established, with large banks such as HDFC, ICICI and SBI all offering appropriate gateways.

Constraints: Consumer acceptance. Consumer acceptance of "non-face-to-face" purchase is relatively low.

Constraints: Broadband penetration. Penetration of broadband (256K) into large Metros is now significant, and at least in Metros is no longer a constraint. Outside of the big cities, it remains an obstacle to effective eCommerce.

Why is there an opportunity? We have a large range of mid-price jewellery which can be sold as a commodity without "touch and feel" selling. The progress of eBay India is a strong indicator of the opportunity. Many constraints have now been removed, and it is therefore believed that a real first-mover opportunity exists in this space. With the exception of YYYY, there is no other player with the nationwide reach or resources to quickly dominate this space.

17.2.3 Fragmented Market

In some ways this is the ideal situation. The "perfect" market for an online proposition is one with a strong mail-order (or telesales) heritage, but where the mail-order players have not generally become multichannel yet. Consumers are used to distance buying, infrastructure such as delivery capability generally exists, but possibly for single-issue reasons such as access to broadband, internet has not become a preferred channel. Alternatively the market can be fragmented, or dominated by niche players, usually small online pure-play start-ups. This is frequently the situation in "simple to start" categories, such as consumer electronics, in emerging online countries. Suggested assessment template with example:

Market: UK professional catering equipment

Addressable **market size**: approximately GBP 650M

Growth: approximately 11% per year

General landscape: a very fragmented market. The only scale player is XXXX.

Key competitor #1: XXXX. Differentiated by Experience, Range and Convenience. *Experience*: A bricks'n'clicks'n'flicks offer including telephone ordering, with a strong mail order heritage. *Range*: A big book catalogue is published twice a year with 50,000 listed SKUs. *Convenience*: Very aggressive convenience promise based around next day delivery.

Other competitors: fragmented players operating in very narrow specialist niches.

In reality there is not so much data which can be captured for assessment in this situation. The key difference from previous templates is the focus on <u>addressable</u> market. Niche players may well operate in extreme niches, such as very local geographies or extraordinarily specialised categories, which will therefore be exceptionally difficult for you to address even with an endless aisle. Excluding such extreme cases, an ideal market, will consist of mail-order, telesales and similar, where it is possible to compete through superior multichannel behaviour, plus basic online pure-plays who may struggle to compete with a more sophisticated player. Some approximation is inevitable. The potential sales opportunity is in any case more likely to be identified by looking at specific existing players and "taking" a share of their sales from them (see the Predator model below).

17.3   Assessing the Sales Opportunity

Three very simple models are provided here to use as a starting point.

Comparative fair-share: intended primarily for highly developed markets – essentially it looks for justification as to why you should end up with more/less than the same share online as you currently have offline;

Predator: intended either for undeveloped markets or for start-ups seeking to take share off existing players;

Bottom-up: intended primarily for fragmented markets or where other reasonable top-down models are not appropriate

17.3.1 Comparative fair-share

This is a two stage model. In the first stage, we simply calculate what a fair share of the new channel (online/eCommerce) market would look like for your target market or categories, starting from the assumption that you capture the same market share online as you currently do offline.

Our share of the offline market / total size of the offline market = our fair share %.

Forecast (or current) online market size * our fair share % = our expected online fair share.

For example, if the offline market is worth 500M and you have sales of 25M, then you have a 5% share. If the online market is estimated to be worth 40M, then your 5% fair share of it will be worth 2M.

In the second stage, we simply look to justify why you might be entitled to more or less of your fair share. The basis proposed is the P.R.I.C.E. differentiation model described in *Chapter 4* and onwards (*Figure 34*).

Our fair share online	Price versus competitors	Range versus competitors	Information versus competitors	Convenience versus competitors	Experience versus competitors	PRICE Summary	Fair Share multiplier	Our sales opportunity
5M	Green	Amber	Amber	Green	Amber	GREEN	2.5	12.5 M
5M	Amber	Red	Red	Green	Red	RED	0.5	2.5M
5M	Green	Amber	Red	Green	Amber	AMBER	1	5M

Figure 34 - Fair Share Assessment Template Stage 2

Step 1: Grade (RAG) the proposed eCommerce proposition against the 5 key differentiators: Price, Range, Information, Convenience, Experience. RAG is not complex: **Green**: better than most competitors (for our target customers); **Amber**: about the same as most competitors; **Red**: not as good as most competitors.

Step 2: summarise the 5 RAG-grades into a single summary RAG.

Step 3: Uplift or reduce the fair-share opportunity according to the summary RAG: **Green**: you will be able to take significantly more than your fair share; **Amber**: you will only take your fair share (at best); **Red**: you will not take your fair share, and 50% is a very(!) optimistic default multiplier.

Step 4: Identify the resulting sales opportunity

There is no especially numerical basis proposed for summarising the differentiation, and although one could be built I suspect it would be rather arbitrary even by the standards of these tools. Similarly the proposed multipliers, suggesting that a better (green) differentiation should entitle you to two-and-a-half times your fair share while a worse (red) differentiation should entitle you to only half are also completely arbitrary although not unreasonable.

As always with these kinds of "consultant" models, the point is in the process and rationalisation of your thought processes, not in the actual direct outcome of the model itself, without further business thinking, experience and judgment applied to it.

17.3.2 Predator

A similar but rather simpler process is proposed for the predator model. The same differentiation assessment is applied, but to the specific competitor's business, as illustrated in *Figure 35.* Again the assumption of capturing 25%/5%/1% of a competitor target's sales when differentiation is rated green/amber/red is arbitrary.

Target	Target sales	Price versus competitor	Range versus competitor	Information versus competitor	Convenience versus competitor	Experience versus competitor	PRICE Summary	Expected share of target's sales	Our sales opportunity
Brand X	50	Green	Amber	Amber	Green	Amber	GREEN	25%	12.5M
Brand Y	100	Amber	Green	Green	Green	Red	AMBER	5%	5M
Brand Z	200	Red	Red	Red	Green	Amber	RED	1%	2M

Figure 35 - Predator Assessment Template

An obvious, but sometimes easy to forget, point is that the competition is allowed to fight back! You will not instantly capture the share you identify: typically it might take 5 years or more. During this time, your competitors will also be developing their offering and business model.

17.3.3 Bottom up

In this situation there are no obvious large-scale benchmark figures such as existing brick-and-mortar or predator-target businesses to use as a baseline. It is therefore necessary to proceed customer-segment by customer-segment. Some care is needed in modelling new channel behaviour based on existing behaviour: customers may not purchase in the same way online as they do offline. For example online may be for distress purchases or specialised items while brick-and-mortar remains for regular large purchases.

Five different customer behaviour changes are suggested here, but of course in reality the number of possibilities is endless:

Increased frequency: increased frequency of shop by existing customers; brick-and-mortar customers use a new channel for additional purchases. Estimate the number of additional checkouts per year per customer, and the expected online cart-size. Note that online carts may be different from offline carts, depending on the mission statements you have associated with your personas (see *Chapter 10*).

Increased cart-size: increased size of shop; brick-and-mortar customers transfer a portion of their spending to a new channel (cannibalisation) but at the same time spend more when doing so. For example this might be a consequence of offering a larger assortment online.

New customers locally: new customers in current segments from the existing catchment areas of your brick-and-mortar stores.

New customers in new geographies: new customers in current segments but from outside your current store catchment areas (obviously a particularly good target for an online offer).

New customers in new segments: totally new customer segments not covered by the previous classifications.

17.4   Ramp-up / Phasing

Obviously no new business reaches its sales targets overnight. Nevertheless, new channel propositions can grow remarkably quickly, and behaviour changes by customers in response can be surprisingly fast. Amazon isn't exactly an old established company, but its sales are over USD 40 Bn worldwide, with some startling year-on-year growth figures.

I'm conscious that it's rather meaningless to propose numbers, but for completeness I suggest a default ratio of 1:2:4:7:10 over the first 5 years, just as a starting assumption, based on a few business cases I've worked on with clients. Having put this into your spread-sheets, overwrite it with something better founded on your own evaluation as soon as possible.

17.5   Top Takeaways

Multichannel does *not* create new money in customers' wallets. A new channel will inevitably cannibalise existing ones. When considering going online, if you don't cannibalise yourself, someone else will do it for you. Therefore it is legitimate to treat *all* forecast online sales as incremental.

Three standard situations are suggested for assessing the competitive landscape: highly developed online, undeveloped online, fragmented.

Three models are proposed for assessing the sales opportunity, using the P.R.I.C.E. framework: comparative fair-share, predator, bottom-up. The bottom-up model is further subdivided into increased frequency, increased cart-size, new customers locally, new customers new geography, new customer segments.

Growth may be fast but won't be instantaneous; a ramp-up phasing model is required.

Chapter 18.   Online Marketing

18.1   Top Down Benchmarks

Unsurprisingly this is an area where public domain data is fairly difficult to source, especially for a "starting out" operation: online pure-play start-ups are not big enough to be required to publish this data, multichannel players don't separate it out in their accounts. However the larger pure-plays do sometimes publish useful benchmarks, and so it is possible to use these as a starting point. Amazon for instance, in its most recent 10-K, shows that marketing spending was 3.8% of turnover.[71] Asos quotes a figure of approximately 4%.[72] These figures are not wildly out of line with what a "typical" (if there is such a thing) brick-and-mortar retailer might spend.

The benchmark planning assumption for an online start-up, which of course also needs to therefore build awareness and brand, is typically a minimum 17% of first year turnover, while a multichannel player might budget 7% of first year turnover in the new channel, with the premium being spent on creating awareness of the new channel.

Traditionally, if it is possible to use such a word in connection with disciplines less than 20 years old, this budget would be spent on a mixture of any/all of the following: search engine optimisation (SEO); search engine marketing (SEM); other pay-per-click / pay-per-impression (PPC, PPM) activities; affiliate marketing; price comparison engine enrolment; social network marketing; eMail or SMS marketing; others. *It would be possible to write several complete books on each of these disciplines. Consistent with my aim of producing a more comprehensive, but inevitably therefore less deep, guide, each is introduced briefly in turn in a section below.*

However, tradition is fine, but unfortunately it ain't so simple.

---

[71] Amazon.com inc, form 10-K, for fiscal year ending 31st December 2011
[72] Asos plc, annual accounts 2011-12

18.2   Logistics is the new Marketing

A steadily developing trend in online retailing is subsidised, or even free, delivery. *Figure 36* shows data captured from a number of leading European websites.

	Standard Shipping Charge	Free shipping on large carts?	Large article shipping charge
Tesco Direct	£3	No	£7
John Lewis	£3	Yes	Free
Boots	£2.95	Yes	£13
Asos	free	n/a	n/a
Debenhams	£3.99	Yes	Free
Marks & Spencer	£3.99	No	Free
Argos	£3.95	No	£8

	Standard Shipping Charge	Free shipping on large carts?	Large article shipping charge
Otto.de	€5,95	No	€ 26
Baur	€5,95	No	€ 40
Conrad	€5,95	Yes	n/a
Rossman	€3,95	Yes	n/a
Goertz	Free	n/a	n/a
Redcoon.de	€5,99	No	€ 40
Notebooksbilliger.de	€5,99	No	€ 40

	Standard Shipping Charge	Free shipping on large carts?	Large article shipping charge
LaRedoute	€5,95	No	n/a
3Suisses	€5,95	No	€ 19
Carrefour Electrical	€6,99	No	€ 60
Auchan Electrical	€4,00	No	€ 65
Etam.fr	€5,90	Yes	n/a
Darty.fr	€5,00	Yes	Free
Galleries Lafayette	€6,60	Yes	n/a

Key: At Cost   Subsidised

Figure 36 - Delivery Charges on Leading European Websites[73]

Partially or fully subsidised shipping is increasingly a feature, especially in the UK which tends to lead trends in online behaviour. Particularly noticeable in the UK is the trend to offer free shipping even on larger (and therefore expensive to ship) articles. Worldwide, Amazon Prime is both well established and increasingly copied. Obviously this comes at a cost. So who should pay for this? Returning to both Amazon and Asos again as leading examples of pure-plays who also conveniently publish accessible accounts, they both tell us the answer:

"While costs associated with Amazon Prime memberships and other shipping offers are not included in marketing expense, we view these

---

[73] Data researched during October 2012

offers as effective worldwide marketing tools, and intend to continue offering them indefinitely."[74]

OK, they don't actually include it in the quoted marketing spend as such, but quite clearly it is considered to be marketing. How much marketing? Excluding services such as marketplace or hosting which clearly don't require shipping, Amazon spends approximately 6% of turnover on these "worldwide marketing tools" (shipping fee income of USD 1.5 Bn, shipping costs of USD 3.9 Bn, net USD 2.4 Bn on USD 40 Bn of "goods" sales). So suddenly instead of 3.8% of sales, Amazon appears to be spending 9.8% of sales on marketing.

Asos is even more explicit:

"From 1 April 2011, the Group has reclassified delivery costs from cost of sales to operating expenses to reflect their increasing deployment as a marketing expenditure. Prior year comparatives have been reclassified accordingly."[75]

Although not quite so dramatic as Amazon, the net effective marketing spend becomes almost 7%, not just the 4% directly associated with the marketing budget. And of course it isn't just pure-plays that are doing this, as the tables in **Figure 36** show. Moreover it is extremely unusual (and I would suggest, also counterproductive) for retailers offering click-and-collect to charge for it, even when the associated parcels are still shipped to store and therefore incur shipping charges (see click-and-collect in **Chapter 26**).

18.3   SEO

As a child I was frequently given copies of the annual Guinness Book of Records as a Christmas present. Its style and language have subsequently modernised, but the 1977 edition[76] still lurking on my bookshelves remains memorable for the following choice of phraseology:

---

[74] Amazon.com inc, form 10-K, for fiscal year ending 31st December 2011
[75] Asos plc, annual accounts 2011-12
[76] Twenty third edition, ISBN 0 900424 37 0

"No single subject is more obscured by vanity, deceit, falsehood and deliberate fraud than..."

And this was written twenty years before SEO was invented! (Actually the quotation then ends "...*the extremes of human longevity.*") Search Engine Optimisation is the gentle art of getting your site to appear at the top of the results of a search-engine query. At least it should be a gentle art, with maybe a small dollop of science. Unfortunately it has been through a protracted iteration of pseudo-science, with a whole sub-industry concentrated on "gaming" the search-engines by second-guessing the rules used to prioritise query results and then modifying sites in artificial ways aligned with these rules. The search-engines, most especially Google, are now fighting back and steadily making these gaming approaches ineffective, and a back-to-basics approach is increasingly likely to be more useful.

What does back-to-basics look like? Essentially it consists of getting some key hygiene factors in place, things that make it easy for the search engines to scan your site; this is the small dollop of science. And then it consists of a lot of hard work, creating and maintaining original and relevant content, product descriptions etc; the gentle art. Search engines are increasingly rewarding this hard work by moving you up the results rankings, which is anyway what they were always aiming to do in the first place – relevant results from relevant content.

Why is it so important? Although the percentage of shopping missions that start from a search page is slowly eroding, a lot still do. If you are my hypothetical example retailer ChoxBox from **Chapter Chapter 10***,* and a customer starts by typing "chocolate gifts" into Google, then being top of the results list is a huge advantage. There are slightly varying data on how big an advantage, but roughly the curve looks like **Figure 37.** Some key takeaways are that the number #1 rank gets more click-throughs than ranks #2, #3, #4 combined, and that it is fairly useless being on the second page or below (although actually being top of page 2 is marginally better than being bottom of page 1).

Figure 37 - Google Search Click-Through Rates[77]

Having I hope demonstrated the importance of SEO, I will very briefly touch on its core techniques –despite asserting that it will continue to become a less technique-based discipline. A practical recommendation is that you should consult an SEO specialist... having first listened to whether he/she focusses on artificial gaming-style approaches or more natural, and more intelligible(!), methods, and made your selection of specialist accordingly. A reasonable investment in SEO can have a far stronger business case than any other marketing technique available, especially if you are small niche player without an existing strong brand, but beware of it becoming an end in itself. It is very much a discipline where 80/20 thinking should apply.

18.3.1 SEO Basic Hygiene

Bluntly, if whoever builds your website doesn't get the technical basics in place, then find someone else. These include ensuring that every page has header tags, titles and meta-descriptions which are linked to content, with relevant and short-as-possible urls. Since any retail site will consist of a lot of product pages, as far as possible these should be generated automatically and consistently. Similarly if your site is too slow for the crawlers/spiders which the search engines use

---

[77]   See   for   example   data   from   Optify, http://searchenginewatch.com/article/2049695

to read your content (which will kill any customer usage of it anyway), or it is not architected with links that they can easily follow from page to page, then find another supplier. And if you find your site stuffed with hidden keywords, then not only find another supplier but sue the previous one.

Content basics are also straightforward: the content needs to be consistently relevant to its topic, and contain key phrases and words that customers are likely to search for. It must not be artificial, as the search engines will penalise this. So it is no good having your brand as every second word in a large amount of hidden content, nor is it (usually!) helpful to write pages including hot keywords like sex when you actually sell furniture or vegetables. If an SEO "expert" recommends buying links, having search-engine-only pages (i.e. not intended for humans), spamming blogs and other content with back-links to your site, or other dubious techniques, find another expert. Search engines now routinely penalise such methods.

18.3.2 Natural SEO

SEO techniques are focussed on what is known as "natural" search i.e. the standard searching process and consequent results that a normal customer would follow, without any bias due to paid sponsorship. Search engines increasingly natural content with natural search priority. Content needs to be new, fresh, original, in depth, frequently updated, contain content relevant to both the rest of the site and the specific page. In other words, it requires continuous hard work.

As is well known, since it was what originally made Google's algorithms stand out in a crowded field in the early days, a major contribution to the ranking of your site and pages is driven by the links to it from other respected sites: respected, quality sites, not link farms. Links from other respected sites are driven primarily by having content which is worth linking to.

If you operate in multiple countries, or even, as search gets ever more sophisticated, in multiple regions, then localised or locality-specific content also helps. For English-speaking and/or European readers its worth remembering too that it isn't just Google (95% of the European search market and around 70% of the US) and Microsoft Bing. Yandex (Russian / Cyrillic) and Baidu (Chinese) dominate their local markets for example. (They certainly spider my own website, which I have just had translated into Russian as an experimental response.)

18.4 SEM

SEO and natural search is nice because it is "free" – well apart from all the effort you need to put in creating suitable content, specialist consultancy you need to pay for, and IT work to present your sites in the right format. By contrast Search Engine Marketing is explicitly not free – you are paying the appearance money to the search engines. Take a look at this desktop screenshot (*Figure 38*).

Figure 38 - Google Search Results – shaded areas are paid adverts

The shaded areas are the SEM paid-for areas. Not a lot of space is left for the natural results, an observation which possibly explains the statistics in the SEO section above. There are in fact only two natural results visible on the page, and people are notoriously reluctant to scroll "below the fold" (I've seen data points as high as 87% of people never scroll below the fold, depending on the type of page in question). The rest of it is entirely SEM results, although to be fair there is some additional bias due to choosing a Christmas gift search term ("Chocolate Gifts") during the Christmas gift-buying season. The effect is even more obvious when I try the same search on my mobile (*Figure 39*):

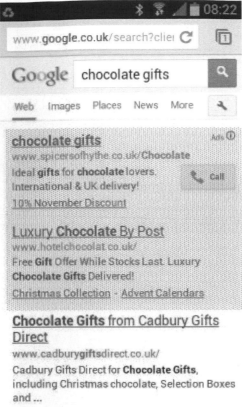

Figure 39 - same search on smartphone, shaded areas are paid-for

We'll discuss mobile in its own chapter later (*Chapter 25*), but just to observe briefly here that increasingly the "research" phase of purchasing is drifting towards mobile devices, even if the eventual completion of the purchase still takes place on another channel. When two thirds of the results are SEM results and only one third SEO, then it gives some idea of Google's revenue strategy, and therefore the potential cost implications for the retailer pursuing search-based marketing in general. Just for interest, the estimated cost per click (CPC) of buying a top 2 ranking in the UK results for "chocolate gifts" was around GBP 2.50 on the day I did this test, which is a large bite out of the gross margins even for products like gift chocolates, especially when you remember that most clicks don't lead to a conversion.

Note the preferred CPC measure. Conventionally online advertising is measured (and charged) in units of:

CPM: cost per thousand impressions

CPC: cost per click-through

CPA: cost per action (usually the "action" is a checkout, although of course this is technically quite complex to actually capture and measure)

For retailers online CPM advertising is generally considered almost irrelevant; it might have some purpose if you simply need to build the brand, but with the much better CPC also available, most retailers focus on CPC-based targets. The technical challenges in tracking CPA, theoretically the "best" measure of effectiveness, tend to confine it to affiliate marketing (see below).

Unlike other forms of marketing CPC also has the benefit of being directly measurable. You can see which keywords work and which don't, and this feedback is often statistically significant after quite short periods of time. A plan-do-review-refine/re-plan methodology should therefore be adopted, aiming to continuously improve the effectiveness of SEM spending (*Figure 40*).

Figure 40 - classic plan-do-review cycle

Although this may not look like much of an insight, it is important to stress the difference with offline activities. Online, it is possibly to quickly, accurately and directly measure the success of any change with genuine confidence that the results are statistically valid (see also website A/B testing in the section on Analytics below - section **21.5**). This is particularly true of SEM; typically clients I have worked with run the complete plan-plan cycle every 2-4 weeks.

18.5 Other pay-per-click activities

Not all customer journeys start from a search engine. Of course best of all, you have such a strong brand that they will start directly on your website. Most retailers are less lucky (or even if they are so fortunate, half the visits will be price-comparison visits anyway), and their customers start on another site. It may therefore make sense to have links from that site. If you sell cameras, and there is a leading online camera magazine, then it's probably a fairly good place to advertise.

Traditionally, that alarming word again when it comes to such young disciplines, an affiliate marketing scheme (see next section) would be the best way to tackle this. There are a number of reasons why you might not prefer this approach. Firstly, affiliate marketing is relatively expensive. Secondly it has a slightly questionable reputation on which you will need to form your own view. Thirdly, and perhaps most interestingly, the rise of mobile – with its great place to research, poor place to checkout status at present – makes it worthwhile driving traffic to your site even if it does not immediately lead to conversion/checkout: there is increasing value in capturing the customer at the research stage.

There are also various alternative networks, in addition to search engines and affiliate-marketing themselves, whose business is to place adverts on a network third-party sites (from which the third-party earns revenue) and then derive revenue when customers click-through to your site. As with the search-engines, their revenue improves as they optimise the placement of such adverts across their partner network, so they have a strong incentive to be effective.

18.6   Affiliate Marketing

As discussed in the SEM section above, CPA – cost per action – is the most attractive way to measure marketing. For a retailer, the desired customer action is a checkout, or even better a series of checkouts. Marketing spending that leads directly from spend to checkout, via a proven and verifiable chain of customer events, is self-evidently well-targeted. Online retail gives you the technical means to make this direct link. Firstly let's look quickly at how it works. It's easiest to start by looking at from the perspective of the affiliate, not the retailer. Theoretically it couldn't be easier (*Figure 41*):

Figure 41 - affiliate marketing, from the affiliate's perspective

Amazon Associates is by far the best known such programme, and (summarising a rather complicated structure) pays the affiliate different commissions by category, varying from 4% to 10% of the transaction value. The Amazon scheme works particularly well for them because they are able to leverage a huge number of niche microsites proposing correspondingly niche-interest books and media; there is a strong correspondence between the customer interests and their likely propensity to purchase items connected to that interest. Other similar and fairly visible schemes outside of retail include those operated by online gambling sites of various kinds, which typically pay a percentage of the turnover of any new victim you persuade to sign-up to them by linking from your "predicting horse racing results using biorhythms and star signs" niche microsite. So far so simple.

Where it all gets a bit messy is when the checkout does not immediately follow the action (click-through from the link). What happens if an affiliate draws a customer to your site, who browses, adds to cart, but then doesn't checkout until the next visit? And then in the meantime a different affiliate also attracts that same customer, who adds another item to their cart, but still doesn't checkout? You will almost certainly have to use an affiliate management partner, who should have various solutions in place to manage this. Nevertheless not all retailers think it worthwhile to give away commission for a customer who might well have arrived there anyway by cheaper means. Asos.com rather famously closed its generally open affiliate programme, and restarted it as a more controlled, invitation only affair, accompanying this change with a memorably rude quote from its CEO:

"I'm not saying we couldn't do more in the online marketing space. Next year we'll reintroduce affiliate marketing, but as it should be. No silly commissions being paid to grubby little people in grubby studios growing income at our expense, getting in the way of genuine sales."[78]

Affiliate marketing can be very effective indeed, but you have to make a decision whether or not it is a) appropriate; b) controllable and

---

[78] http://econsultancy.com/uk/blog/918-affiliates-close-rank-after-asos-ceo-calls-them-grubby

manageable; c) available as a technical solution in your locale; d) affordable in your market and categories (I still have a vivid memory of explaining the concept to an Indian client who had not previously encountered it, and watching jaws hit the table when I mentioned the usual levels of commission and consequent implied lost gross margin). Unlike SEO and SEM, it should not be an automatic choice.

18.7   Price Comparison Engines

The top price comparison sites draw a huge amount of traffic. A top of listing spot for a hot ticket item will attract a large percentage of that traffic to you. But... you have to pay for it twice. Firstly, although the commercial models of course vary, price comparison is essentially a variation on affiliate marketing. The engine has to earn its money from somewhere, and this is either from retailer or brand advertising, retailer subscriptions, or direct commissions. You are probably paying either affiliate-style or SEM-style for the privilege of your share of all this traffic. Secondly, you then have to be amongst the cheapest anyway. Unless you already have a price advantage, there is a double cost.

In extreme cases, the cost is so great that the opposing business model applies: retailers make an effort to block price comparison sites from harvesting their online prices. In general this is a futile battle that you are almost certain to lose, by technical means anyway. Nevertheless, active engagement with price comparison sites generally has a net positive cost-benefit case only to those retailers with a stable price advantage in the first place. Otherwise, you may have no choice but to be a passive victim, but don't deliberately solicit (and pay for!) victimisation.

18.8   Social Network Marketing

Writing this section makes me nervous. Which is a sign of my belief in the power of social networks. They seem to have the power to start revolutions, lose elections, and create celebrities overnight. As a way to promote your brand, and as a traffic driver to your website, they can be tremendously effective. But...

Q: what comes after ⓔ-commerce

A: f-commerce

Figure 42 - already an old joke?

As a *direct* driver of *online* retail sales, their case is at best unproven. It hasn't really happened. Maybe that sentence should finish with the word "yet", but the evidence just isn't there.

Before any social marketing specialists start posting blisteringly scathing reviews and giving this book one-star ratings on Amazon – another sign of the power of social – I'd just like to make it clear: social marketing undoubtedly has a place in a retailer's marketing activities portfolio. The problem is that, unlike other techniques that lead in a directly measurable straight-line to the bottom line such as SEO, SEM, or email marketing, social marketing is more akin to pure advertising – an indirect driver. Even compared to pure advertising, where there is (hopefully!) a visible effect in response to a defined campaign, social marketing is more diffuse: it's about gradually building long term relationships with customers which simply don't generate observable large-scale step-changes in sales. It is very difficult to demonstrate a simple and direct cause-and-effect relationship in the way that other tools can. The problem is not that social marketing is a weak tool, more that other techniques are so self-evidently powerful in an online environment, where measurement on a transaction-by-transaction basis is so easy. However once you consider the wider picture, a genuinely multichannel proposition again, with the majority of sales taking place in stores where direct causality is much harder to measure, social marketing moves back into its rightful place nearer the top of the queue for spending. A long-term relationship with a customer is indeed a precious thing (and incidentally upon which many retailers are able to place a quantified value, which is then a good basis for a business case for social marketing).

As I write this, I am reading statistics published by IBM about 2012 thanksgiving holiday-weekend sales in the US, which includes the following quote:

"Less strong, however, is so-called 'social shopping' — that is, retail being driven via social network referrals on sites like Facebook, Twitter, and Pinterest. This, so far, has only generated online sales of 0.2%"[79]

The key word in this (fairly typical) quote is "referrals" — their focus is on immediately measurable impacts, not on longer term. This whole part of the book is primarily targeted at the tasks involved in going online in the first place, and in that specific situation I would argue that social marketing should not be a high priority. Once the goal of getting online is accomplished and the next challenge – becoming truly multichannel – is faced, social marketing should definitely move up the charts.

18.9   eMail marketing

It would be possible to write a complete book on email marketing, and a glance at Amazon shows that plenty of people have done so. So, to address the challenge of summarising several books into a concise sub-chapter, how about a memorable acronym? Email marketing should be TART: Timely; Actionable; Relevant; Triangular. I'll take a brief look at each of these points in turn, with a particular focus on their specific application to retail.

18.9.1 Timely

Firstly, customers have often actually asked you for emails. For example, customers like to be updated about the status of their orders, and will agree to these emails even if they opt out of others. It is important to deliver this information to reduce the number of expensive calls to your contact-centre anyway, but it is also a perfectly

---

[79]http://techcrunch.com/2012/11/22/ibm-thanksgiving-sales-data-shows-mobile-commerce-jumping-iphoneipad-driving-19-of-traffic-social-nets-only-0-2/

legitimate marketing opportunity. Don't let the marketing obstructing the information the customer wanted - such an email should be roughly "here is your information, by the way what about..." in structure – and don't expect fantastic take-up, but nevertheless don't miss the opportunity. The customer wants to be communicated with, you know exactly who the customer is (see *relevant* below), you can propose something they might have a high propensity to want, even if it's only the cross-sell products for their ordered items that they maybe didn't take up when you first suggested them on the website.

Secondly, there are moments when it is both very effective and also reasonably legitimate to jump down a customer's throat with an email. The best-known is probably cart-abandonment. If you observe a cart built, but then not checked-out in a reasonably timely manner, send that customer an encouraging email. When this is both well-timed and appropriate, conversion rates can be spectacular. I'd like to quote a data point with a reference, but they are either client confidential or dubiously biased because they are quoted by suppliers of email marketing solutions; so as an unreferenced data-point assumption for planning, well-executed cart-abandonment emails have approximately 6-times higher conversion rates than a default "blast" email. Note how important timing is here. The average first-site-visit-to-purchase journey time is around 18-19 hours. The cart-to-checkout part of that is less than half. If you jump on the customer in the middle, especially when they are just using the cart as a holding area for products in their consideration-set, you'll probably put them off. Leave it too long, and you won't get the benefit. As with all things online, the fact that you can directly measure means that constant experimentation and tuning is the key to success (**Figure 40** again).

Anecdotally illustrating the pitfalls of these techniques, Amazon have developed a flavour of this which could be described as "browse abandonment": they notice when I have looked at a category without purchasing, and then start emailing me about it. As this is invariably after I have been using them either as a price comparison site, or to take a screenshot to illustrate a point to a client, it is distinctly counter-productive to the extent that the only reason I don't relegate their emails to my spam-filter is that I have a professional interest in following their methods.

And with spam-filters firmly in mind, thirdly, there is a good ol' regular email blast. Most of the success factors for these lie in the other areas to be discussed shortly, but timing still plays its part. An empirical approach is still the best. For example, split your customers into random groups, and try twice-weekly, weekly, bi-weekly and measure the take-up. Similarly, try different times of day (a nice study suggested that the early hours of Sunday night works best in the UK, aiming for the Monday-morning inbox) and measure the response.

Fourthly, and better than the simple blast, if you have relevant news, such as a sale event, of course tell customers about it. The increasing number of successful private-sale sites are particularly dependent on this approach; the customer, by subscribing to such a private-sale club, has effectively requested such emails, and of course are much more likely to open a mail they have asked for than an unsolicited one. Even if your business model is more conventional, emails about a genuine sale event with real benefits for the customer will have far better take-up than just another deal.

18.9.2 Actionable

Firstly the Actionable you don't want: in many (most) countries, there is legislation requiring customers to opt-in to emails before you start sending them. Don't forget to capture this opt-in in any interaction where you ask customer's for an email address. A big database of contactable customers that you are not legally permitted to contact is extremely frustrating, although not as frustrating as a big pile of lawyers' letters complaining when you did contact them without permission. Of course you can choose to ignore this, but at your brand's peril. (And even if you are just trying to make a quick buck, it is exactly the kind of thing even basic due-diligence processes look at when you try to sell the business, precisely because it's such obvious territory for lawyers).

The Actionable you do want is your customers doing something positive in response to your emails – opening them, preferably clicking-through to a website, and then doing something good when they get there. The opening step is dealt with under *triangular* below. The next step is clicking through. It is genuinely astonishing how many emails don't get this simple step right: it needs to be obvious where to click to get what response. Remember our One Second Rule from the introductory chapters? For emails, you are very lucky if you even get one second. Don't make the customer actually have to read it like Sherlock Holmes, put things in it that scream "click here" at them. I won't give examples, because there are hundreds and hundreds online; check a few of them out.

The second part is that the click-through has to arrive at the intended landing-page. Make sure your landing page url is statically named (i.e. your IT system does not dynamically generate a new temporary url every time the page is accessed). And when the customer arrives, measure and record it, because you will need this data for the next email you send out.

18.9.3 Relevant

I'm talking to you.

Not just a generic you, but specifically you the individual. Personalisation is a critical topic for multichannel, and therefore discussed at length in its own *Chapter 24* below. I'll use a very simple example now to illustrate the point. Suppose your website sells wine. You know that I have occasionally bought red wine from it, but never white wine. Should you send me an email with a white wine offer?

18.9.4 Triangular

There are a bunch of best practice guidelines to follow when preparing emails. For example titles should be as short as possible, three-to-five words being optimal. The guideline which gives this section its title is that the body of an email should also be a tapering triangle like this (*Figure 43*) for maximum impact and response.

Figure 43 - The perfect shape for an email?

At least, several experts on the topic have assured me that this is so. I haven't yet met an Arabic (or other right-to-left language) expert who can confirm that this behaviour should be mirrored in these cultures.

I picked this particular guideline as an illustration of something that might well be unexpected. The point is that there is a tremendous pool of knowledge available, either online or via appropriate consultants, in this particular space. The "rules" are not necessarily intuitively obvious, since they rely on bizarre human psychological responses, and have generally been learned empirically by practitioners. I am not, in this book, going to be able to cover such a specialist topic in depth, and therefore in this particular space, rather like SEO, I recommend strongly that you consult a domain expert, of which there are many.

18.10 SMS marketing

Having found a memorable acronym (TART) to define the approach you should take to email marketing, I have spent some time trying to find one suitable for describing what should happen with SMS marketing. Alas, considerable cogitation has failed to inspire me with anything that the letters B.A.N.N.E.D. could stand for.

OK, this is not really fair. The problem with SMS is that it can be extremely effective. Why is this a problem? Because its effectiveness is achieved via intrusiveness and generates subsequent resentment.

With a huge health-warning around the validity of these statistics, a quick comparison of SMS with email (*Figure 44*):

	eMail[80]	SMS
Open rate	Up to 38% (if you are very lucky)	Up to 98%
Click-thru rate	Averages between 10-22%	Approx 15-20%
Conversion rate	Averages between 1-3%	Up to 16%

Figure 44 – Dubious comparison of eMail and SMS marketing

Just to repeat, these statistics are extremely suspect, especially those for SMS. They depend entirely on circumstances, content, brand, purpose, target and a thousand-and-one other factors. The only practical way to determine the effectiveness of such campaigns for your business is to try them, and establish some baselines. The basic message is that SMS is a more powerful tool for getting attention and also for causing irritation, and if your objective is click-throughs then SMS obviously has some challenges, not least the existence of a mobile site to land on.

Unsolicited SMS is not a recipe for commercial success – at least in retail - as anybody who is following the high profile Papa Johns story in the US will be aware. (If you have not seen this, Papa Johns pizza chain is currently facing a USD 250M class action lawsuit as a consequence of an unsolicited SMS marketing campaign).[81] However, there are legitimate solicited SMS situations: providing updates on order status for example, which of course can also become marketing opportunities. In countries with less developed online infrastructure and where an individual's email addresses can be fickle, SMS might well be a more reliable means of contacting the customer, and in these cultures semi-solicited SMS is generally more acceptable.

---

[80] Various sources, including US Direct Marketing Association
[81] See for example http://money.cnn.com/2012/11/13/technology/mobile/papa-johns/index.html

18.11 Offline

The general principle of online marketing – that almost everything can be measured directly, and therefore should be measured directly – should be very evident. By implication, there is usually an investment in software and/or services required to do it well. Those who provide such services should be experts themselves, and any negotiation with such a potential partner should include obtaining a few free days of consulting on these sometimes very specific specialist topics.

Despite all these wonderfully measurable online methods, and depending on the preferred customer journeys you have identified (see Part A of this book), then offline marketing may still be a very valid option. A particularly common combination – because it is an effective combination – is flicks'n'clicks: combining a paper catalogue with a website (or its multichannel extension flicks'n'clicks'n'bricks... Yeah OK.) Websites, and mobile sites, are good places to search but relatively bad places to browse. If your customer behaviour involves a significant level of browse behaviour, then paper catalogues may well still make a lot of sense. You do need to coordinate the product numbers in the catalogue with what is displayed (and searchable for) on your website, which adds yet another piece of data to capture in that, by now familiar challenge, product data management.

18.12 Top Takeaways

A first-year of operation planning benchmark might be 17% of sales for an online pure-play, or 7% for a multichannel proposition.

Amazon currently spends 3.8% of turnover on marketing. However when shipping offers are included, which Amazon regards as marketing, then this rises to almost 10%. Comparable figures for Asos are 4% and 7%.

Logistics is the New Marketing. Traditional online marketing might include any or all of: search engine optimisation (SEO); search engine marketing (SEM); other pay-per-click activities; affiliate marketing;

price comparison engine enrolment; social network marketing; eMail or SMS marketing; others.

The impact of most online marketing spending is directly measurable. Implement a very frequent plan-do-measure-review cycle.

SEO is an essential discipline. Get the hygiene right, consult a specialist, but remember that engines are increasingly rewarding content in preference to technique.

SEO impact is strongly skewed towards the top few positions.

When planning SEM campaigns, take care to ensure that you get as much benefit as the search engine does.

Cost-per-action is a more direct measure of effectiveness than cost-per-click is a more direct measure than cost-per-thousand-impressions. CPA > CPC > CPM.

Affiliate marketing can be measured by CPA (=good). However managing it effectively is more than usually challenging.

Social media marketing for the retailer does not typically produce directly measurable returns, but it is nevertheless important, especially for multichannel retailers. Other directly measurable options can seem more urgent. Importance and urgency should not be confused.

Email marketing is a very specialist skill. An outline is that it should be TART: timely, actionable, relevant and triangular.

SMS marketing needs to be strongly validated for appropriateness. Unsolicited SMS can have negative consequences.

Data protection legislation is especially applicable online.

Don't omit offline techniques. Bricks'n'clicks'n'flicks can be a powerful mixture. Always relate back to your customer personas and missions.

Chapter 19.   Product Data Management Again

Yes. Again.

19.1   Re-introduction

This part of the book is about getting online in the first place, which usually basically means setting up your website (and related channels of course, such as mobile site). The core customer journeys on websites all begin with either Searching or Browsing. Product master data is at the heart of both of these experiences, and this chapter will look at some of the specifics of making sure they work for customers.

Since we are also using the business case as a structure, just a quick reminder of the basic planning assumption to use - 25 minutes per SKU to obtain and organise the necessary data. As with all benchmark data points, this is only valid until you have your own direct experience. Of course you also need some sort of system to organise it in, which can vary from spreadsheets to multimillion dollar/pound/euro solutions, which is a topic I will cover in the later chapter on IT (*Chapter 21*).

We'll start by browsing.

19.2   Taxonomy

An assortment's taxonomy is NOT product master data. It is a property of *how* you sell, not *what* you sell, and is therefore merchandising (see *Chapter 15*).

Before expanding on that assertion, we need to define the term taxonomy. An assortment's taxonomy is generally identified with the browsing hierarchy that you will be familiar with on any retail website, usually displayed at the top of the screen looking something like *Figure 45* (a display area known technically as a Breadcrumb Trail).

Figure 45 - taxonomy / browsing hierarchy[82]

The most important part of any taxonomy is the Top- or 1st-Level of the hierarchy. In this breadcrumb, the top-level is "Baby". Conventionally - and these conventions increasingly exist because they are proven to work - this top level will be visible on most/all of the key pages on your website. **Figure 46** is a screenshot from the same website, showing the complete top menu section (incidentally notice the prominent "free delivery from 20 Euros" message. See section **18.2**):

Figure 46 - website top menu, showing top level hierarchy[83]

Getting the correct top menu is a key task for any retail website. The reasons for this become particularly clear when we take a look at the same retailer's mobile site (**Figure 47**).

[82] From bol.com, November 2012
[83] ibid

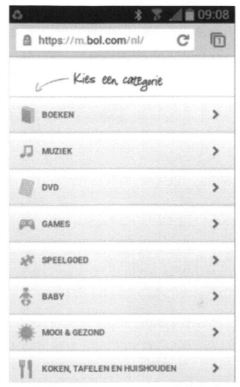

Figure 47 - same taxonomy, mobile channel[84]

Excluding Search, the *only* route into this retailer's assortment is via this short list of words. It follows that organising these categories in the right way is one of the most important tasks for any online retail proposition, and one that tends to get neglected in amongst more exciting possibilities. I would also argue strongly that the moment you decide to launch a mobile site as a companion to your main website is a very good moment to take another look at the efficiency of your taxonomy.

Let's return now to the assertion that taxonomy is *not* product data. There are some sophisticated logical-data-structure arguments behind this which are important, but it is not so easy to demonstrate these convincingly to anyone outside a rather specialist IT-logical-architecture audience. Fortunately there are some much simpler

---

[84] ibid

reasons. The most obvious is that a product may sit in multiple places in a hierarchy. Consider a fashion website, which invites customers to browse both by garment-type (e.g. coats, dresses, trousers) and by brand. Such a site will have *at least* a double hierarchy. If you add in further navigation routes for the customer, such as perhaps a special offers section, it is easy to see that a single product can end up occupying multiple slots in the hierarchy structure. Another reason is that you might have different sales channels with different hierarchies; a specialist clearance site for example, or a branded micro-site.

The implication of such multiple hierarchies lies primarily in the process you should use to manage the taxonomy:

WRONG WAY: make a big table of your products, and then next to each product list its position in the hierarchy;

RIGHT WAY: make a big map - which will look rather like a diagram of a tree - of your hierarchy, and then drop your products onto its "leaves". You can quite easily drop the same product onto several different leaves if that is what is required.

This is not just true when first creating a taxonomy, it's true for managing it ongoing as well. The process should always be 1) define/refine the taxonomy; 2) the taxonomy "pulls" the products onto itself. Do not accept being given processes in which your products "push" themselves into places on the taxonomy by apparently knowing about it by themselves. (Incidentally for smaller retailers using entry-level software solutions, this distinction in process approach is strongly recommended as one of the various ways to tell a good solution + supplier from a bad one). *Figure 48* illustrates the idea.

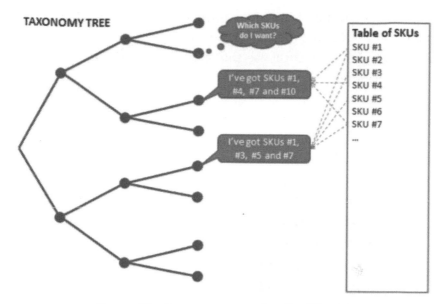

Figure 48 - Taxonomy creation "pull" process

Note that there is (or should be) no requirement that every leaf on the taxonomy has the same depth so products themselves could sit at the 2nd level (Home -> Special Offers) and the 4th level (Home -> Baby -> On the move -> Car Seats) within the same taxonomy. Good practice is to try to ensure that all the leaves have a reasonably consistent number of products in them, typically between 10 and 50. Having one leaf with 1000 products and another with only 3 not only looks silly, but can cause issues with inconsistent site behaviour.

Note also that a retailer's <u>buying</u> hierarchy is almost never a hierarchy which should simply be shown to customers. As a simple example, I worked with a client whose buying hierarchy included the term "dry drinks". In actual fact it meant things like teabags and coffee powder (despite my mental pictures of alcohol-free beer and wine, or in madder moments of powdered water), but it certainly wasn't a term to display to customers. Even simply using a more customer-friendly name is not usually adequate. For example, you might have your buying for a particular category split into domestic and overseas, but you probably don't want to display this distinction to your customers.

There is no simple labour-saving way to avoid creating the taxonomy from scratch and then placing your products one by one, although there will probably be shortcuts at least at sub-sub-category level. Many retailers maintain their taxonomy using index cards on the wall (or floor if they have a lot of products!), which sounds oddly un-technical but seems to be the best way in practice; if you want to use software, you need an extremely large screen.

19.3   Search

Taxonomy is primarily (although not exclusively) about making sure *browse* works for your customers. The other route to your merchandise is *search*. Unlike taxonomy, search definitely is *mainly* about product data. We'll look more into the technology side of search in the IT chapter (**Chapter 21**). What is important to understand here is that the product search and navigation functions on a website do *not* work in the way that say Google, or any other search engine, does. Search engines like Google work by looking "from the outside in", scanning each page that you choose to display. They do not, in general, rely on any structure in what they find – every word, or data point, is equal. Retail website product search, by contrast, works "from the inside out". What does this mean?

Take a look again at **Figure 15,** that loaf of bread. The data about it includes a list of ingredients, one of which is unsurprisingly "flour". What happens on a grocery website if a customer enters the word "flour" in a search box? What you want is a list of packets of flour. What you don't want is a very long list of products which have flour as an ingredient, probably not topped by packets of flour but by various breads and cakes. Simplifying (a lot), an "outside in" search-engine style search will see a lot of text, and with no other guidance, will treat all text as equal, so bread is just as much flour as flour itself is. The "inside out" search used by retail sites is given some more guidance by, or about, the product data. In this particular example, it would be told that text listed as "ingredients" is not as important as text listed as "product name". So when "flour" is entered by the customer, the more relevant products called "flour" are top of the list.

As we head from search towards navigation, consider the same grocery website being contemplated by a customer who has gluten-allergy. The full ingredient listed for that loaf of bread is "wheat flour", which contains gluten. How do you tell this to a search engine? Again the "inside out" engines are given that advantage via either hidden data which is not text (such as a Yes/No flag for gluten-content) and/or extra rules information. So when a customer asks for "gluten free" in a search box, or ticks a "gluten-free" checkbox somewhere in the navigation structure, the engine is aware of the relationship between the ingredient "wheat flour" and the property "gluten free". This is pretty much impossible for a Google-type engine to do reliably; artificial intelligence hasn't yet reached this level, so the implementation reality is invariably extra hidden product data or rules.

19.4   Navigation

Checkboxes for "gluten free" are not strictly search, and more properly lie in the realm of navigation. Once again, product data is the foundation of effective navigation. Take a look at *Figure 49*.

Figure 49 - navigating to the right dress[85]

---

[85] Collage from asos.com, November 2012

This is a part (and only a part) of the navigational features to help you choose the right dress. The site in question sells over 2000 different dresses, so obviously the customer needs plenty of direction to finding the right one. To deliver that direction, every single dress has had its colour, size, shape, brand etc not only entered, but entered *consistently*. For example, there are 19 colours defined in this navigation. A child's box of crayons probably has more than 19 colours in it. To make this navigation work, some strict standards have been defined, for example the one that says that "red" is a valid colour but "scarlet" is not.

Product master data management, and the closely associated merchandising data management, is all about such standards, the processes to manage entry, and constant quality control. It is the foundation of online retailing. It needs a Business Process approach to it. The data identified to describe each sub-sub-category of product you will sell need to be defined. The responsibility, and timeline, for entering this data has to be set out. The process of entering it has to be monitored and quality controlled. I was talking very recently to a company which provides outsourced services to retailers — basically they will run your eCommerce for you. And they had a 124 step process they followed for each product to capture and manage its data. Another client I have worked with directly had a 93 step process. Once you have more than a few hundred SKUs, you can't avoid it, so start planning now. Even more than the IT itself, product data management has been the critical path on every retail website implementation I have ever worked on or heard about. And it isn't just the initial implementation. You need clearly *defined* processes, and except for the very smallest retailers, clearly *documented* processes, for all common use-cases: adding a new product, removing an old one, changing prices, adding promotions, amending the taxonomy, adding a new description, taking a new photo... Because unlike other IT systems or data, you are doing this to a system that your customer are watching and using 24 hours a day, seven days a week, and so any mistake is a very public mistake. Good product data is the main difference between a good website and a poor one. You will reap far more benefit in terms of sales from investing in good product data management than you ever will worrying about whether a particular user-feature would be a good thing to add.

19.5   Simplified Example

I'm keen to stress that word 'simplified' before presenting this example; this is an especially relevant word if some of this data is interfaced from other IT systems. The practical task of managing the data and the properly definition of IT logical data structures to support it can seem quite far apart, and a discussion of IT enterprise architecture considerations is definitely not in scope for this book; some of what follows might therefore make the purist wince. Be that as it may, I already started using dresses as an example, so let's continue on the same theme: a new hypothetical retailer, MegaClothes, selling a party frock from its exciting MegaFrocks range.

Product data is generally specified in attribute-value pairs. For example the attribute might be "weight" and the value might be "400 grammes". Of course nothing is ever quite so simple, and in this case the specification in a real system might be in an attribute-value-unit triple, so the value would be "400" and the unit would be "grammes". I'm keen to keep this example simplified though, so I'm going to avoid (or should that be evade?) these kinds of additional complications.

Attributes are divided into those which are common across all your products – for example "brand" – and those which are specific to a category or sub-category. *Figure 49* showed "dress shape" as one of the attributes of a dress. Clearly this is no use when describing bras, when a cup-size attribute would be relevant instead. For every category, or sub-category, it is necessary to define what category-specific attributes you require. (Applying this to the taxonomy topic, position in taxonomy should *never* be managed as though it were an attribute of the product.)

Some attributes are visible to customers. Others are used internally in various ways: they might be hidden in support of navigation like the "gluten free" example above; they might involve parts of the operation that you don't want to directly display to customers, such as the packaged-weight of the product which you might use to calculate the shipping charge; they might be part of controlling the work-flow of creating and completing the product data itself, such as a QA-sign off without which the product will not be listed on your website. For simplicity I'm going to stick with referring to all of these as attributes, even though in a more complex IT system they might well be managed in quite different ways, especially the work-flow aspects and/or data interfaced from other systems such as price.

We'll look at organisational issues in **Chapter 22** below, but responsibility for collating this information is often spread across your organisation, with a coordinating function adding the specifically "website" parts and performing quality assurance.

NB: **Figure 50** is NOT intended to be a definitive list of all the likely attributes for a dress, just those selected to make illustrative points.

Attribute	Value	Visible/ Internal	Who is responsible	Comment
Common Attributes				
SKU#	12345678	Internal	Buying	
Catalogue number	12-34-56	Visible	Merchandising	Don't use the SKU number for this; you'll find that causes problems later on. You need a number to display on invoices and catalogues
Brand	Megafrocks	Visible	Buying	
Size	12	Visible	Buying	This type of attribute is known as a "variant"; a website will not list ten dresses identical except for size, rather it will list one dress with ten size options
Colour	Black	Visible	Buying	This type of attribute has a

160

					strictly controlled set of valid values, so entering "dark grey" will be rejected – it's either black or grey.
Name	MegaFrocks Little Black Party Frock	Visible	Web team		Coming back to the SEO topic for a moment, the product-page url-name for this frock should include the name if at all possible
Description	Ideal for Xmas parties	Visible	Merchandising		There is often a big process difference between attributes which are "facts" and attributes which are "opinions". For example "opinions" are not usually very high priority for Search.
Shipping weight	400g	Internal	Logistics		
Stock Locations	Warehouses #1 and #3	Internal	Logistics		This type of attribute might be explicitly stated, or it might be "deduced" from the interface with your other logistics systems. This tends to depend on the complexity of your existing brick-and-mortar operation if you have one.
Overseas shipping?	No	Internal	Logistics		
First day on sale	15th November	Internal	Buying		

QA sign-off	Yes	Internal	Web team	Processes are required to make sure you don't "publish" a product to your website until it is completely prepared in all its aspects.
Price	£100	Visible	Buying (note to those who design IT architecture: price is always merchandising data)	Attributes such as price are often sourced "automatically" from the central merchandising systems. It is necessary to put in place processes to ensure the systems stay in synch, and also that the price can be overridden on the web in emergencies.
You may also like	SKU #9876	Visible	Merchandising	Most retailers have to maintain this data manually.
Get the look	SKU #7777 + SKU #6666	Visible	Merchandising	There is no way to avoid maintaining this data manually!
Search priority	2	Internal	Web team (although strictly it is merchandising)	Instructions to your internal search, in this case that it should be high up a list of results but not at the top
New until	15th February	Internal	Merchandising	Instructions to your website itself, in this case that a "New!" splash logo should be displayed next to the image
Images	url-name X	Internal	Buying	Where to look for the main picture of this item

Attributes Specific to Dresses Categories				
Dress shape	Shift	Visible	Buying	
Dress length	Mini	Visible	Buying	

Figure 50 - simplified product data example

As you can see, I have already identified 18 attributes for this simple black party frock just when constructing an artificial illustrative example. Real world situations are usually more complex.

There are some possible external sources of such data. A few companies specialise in providing it for specific categories (BrandBank for branded groceries, for example – as always, no recommendation or otherwise implied. The consumer electronics industry has a free-to-use collaboration called icecat[86], which offers ways to source and manage this data in 35 languages.) You need to carefully evaluate the quality of such sources before enthusiastically subscribing as a way of avoiding all this internal labour. Even if you use an external source, there is still a big organisational task to do; when they work well, they are still not a silver bullet.

19.6   Top Takeaways

Browse and Search are the two main methods customers use to find products on a website.

Taxonomy, usually identified with the assortment browsing hierarchy on a website, is the browsing gateway to your products. Taxonomy is part of merchandising.

A taxonomy should have a root-branch-leaf structure; leaves should be of approximately equal size. It is critical to get the root-level right for customers, especially on mobile sites.

---

[86] See www.icecat.biz

A taxonomy should *never* be defined via product master data attributes. Products should always be "pulled" into a taxonomy; they should never push their own way in.

Existing buying hierarchies are typically inappropriate to map one-for-one into taxonomies.

Internal website search differs from Google-style search; an internal search will receive more data/rules guidance for prioritising its results, be more focussed on merchandising, and be able to access invisible data attributes.

Search and navigation are enabled by product master data and merchandising data. Such data is typically structured in attribute/value pairs such as colour/red. It may be visible or invisible to customers.

The management of this data requires formally defined and documented business processes for all common use-cases, as well as standards for data entry into each attribute.

Good product data is the biggest enabler of a good website instead of a bad one. It does not come cheap.

Chapter 20.   Order Lifecycle

20.1   Definition

This rather bureaucratic-sounding term refers to everything that happens after the wonderful moment when the customer hits that "submit order" button on your checkout. In summary it covers payment, warehousing, pick-pack-ship, returns, (much of) customer-services, and often a lot of financial system tracking. In less officious language it's "getting the stuff to customers that they've paid for".

That there is reasonably close linkage between these elements should be self-evident. Just how closely coupled they are becomes especially plain when you start to consider what happens when something goes wrong. Linking back with the previous chapter for example, what happens when you arrive at the pick-face in your warehouse ready to pick your customer-order, only to find that the last MegaFrocks little black party dress remaining in stock actually has a large rip down the back? Probably you now have to contact the customer, re-price the order, re-price the shipping, re-label the parcel, re-print the invoice, change the shipping company collection manifest, write-off the stock, possibly refund some of the payment... (If you weren't convinced the first time by the urgings in the available-to-promise *Chapter 16* to keep it simple, maybe you are convinced now!).

For mail-order companies, 80% of this stuff is business-as-usual when they go online, which is part of the reason taking mail-order online is usually a relatively simple business model development. For brick-and-mortar retailers, 80% of it is both new and often causes conflict with existing well-established business-processes.

20.2   Payment

20.2.1 Payment Policy

Depending on the market in which you are operating, you will offer various different payment options to your customers. These might range from credit card to bank transfer to cash on delivery. When planning order lifecycle the important thing to define is *when* the payment takes place.

Firstly note that payment card transactions are typically actually a two-stage process. Stage 1, known as "authorisation", is the process of reserving funds against the customer's card. A variety of validation checks will be performed by the various participants in this process, all aimed at ensuring that the card is valid and that the funds are available. The most familiar example of such transactions are when you are asked in hotels to present a credit card at the start of your stay, which will be blocked for a certain pre-reserved amount. Stage 2, known as "capture", actually moves the money from the card to the merchant i.e. pays! If you pay for something over the counter in a store, authorisation usually takes place on the spot, but capture quite often is an overnight process, and the time-lapse generally doesn't matter. Payment Policy is about deciding when authorisation and capture will take place, and applies to non-card transactions by implication as well.

Typically authorisation will take place either during, or immediately after, the website checkout. This is usually fine, but suppose you are selling made-to-order billiard tables, which take 15 weeks to build? It is not reasonable to block a large amount of the customer's card limit for 15 weeks, and in fact generally card companies automatically release authorisations after somewhere between 2 and 5 days anyway. In this situation you would probably prefer to authorise just before shipping. Many websites with this kind delayed payment will typically do a trial authorisation for a small minimum amount during the checkout, whose purpose is essentially just to validate that the card is genuine and has no silly issues such as an expiry date before the likely payment is required.

Payment capture usually takes place at one of three moments: pay-on-order; pay-on-despatch; pay-on-delivery.

Pay-on-order is what you would normally expect to do for an eBay transaction for example, while Amazon generally operates pay-on-despatch. Pay-on-delivery usually means payment on the door-step, but could also mean waiting for the shipping company to confirm the delivery and then executing the capture step.

If your preferred payment method is cash-on-delivery, then your payment policy in general is both obvious and mandatory. For other methods, it is essential to make the choice, stick with it, and accept the consequences throughout the order lifecycle. In the sub-section on returns policy just below, I'll define most of the archetypal situations that need to be considered. There is no "best" or "worse" choice of payment policy, it depends on your business, although in some countries this choice is partially or completely prescribed by the local regulatory system. In general, in all countries you should ensure that you are aware of distance-selling laws, which often give customers additional rights over-and-above what you might be used to in a brick-and-mortar environment. On a similar regulatory note, beware as well of different PCI/DSS-compliance requirements for online transactions[87].

20.2.2 Fraud

Payments on a website are defined as CNP transactions – Customer Not Present or Card Not Present. Most payment schemes charge higher merchant fees for CNP transactions, reflecting the higher risk of fraud and chargeback. The higher your track-record rate of chargebacks, the higher your merchant fees will become. The worst case I have ever seen was a retailer generally paying typical fees of 1.0-2.5% on most in-store transactions which found itself facing proposed fees of 10% online. Such charges will cripple most business models, so it is worth doing something about it proactively.

Firstly Verified-by-Visa[88] and Mastercard Securecode[89] should be implemented by default if you plan to accept credit card payments at all and there is any existing customer acceptance of these schemes in

---

[87] See https://www.pcisecuritystandards.org, although I recommend speaking to a specialist, not wading through the material yourself
[88] See for example http://www.visaeurope.com/en/cardholders/verified_by_visa.aspx
[89] See for example http://www.mastercard.us/securecode.html

your region. Similarly any schemes specific to your country's preferred payment methods should always be implemented. Secondly, have a very hard think about whether or not you want to accept credit cards from overseas. Particularly if you don't ship overseas, the lost business from occasional frustrated expats may well be more than offset by the reduced fraud risk of blocking their cards. Many retailers maintain BIN range (the first 6 digits of the card number) tables defining ranges they find unacceptable, which can be managed at country level, so for example a Belgian site might decide to accept Dutch and French cards, but not Bulgarian ones. Brick-and-mortar retailers also often have private hot-card lists, still sometimes just pinned to the check-out, and these should be uploaded to website checkout if possible.

Finally, there are specialist fraud-prevention solutions available. Complete solutions are generally only worthwhile for larger players, but slightly less specialised solutions are often available from your chosen card payment gateway provider (or payment service provider – PSP - the two terms are more-or-less interchangeable). A PSP is a specialised service that sits as an interface between a website and (normally) your usual acquiring bank. There are slightly different configurations possible, but the outline set-up is shown in *Figure 51.*

Figure 51 - Payment Gateway and Fraud Screening

Many banks, especially in "developing" online retail countries (I have found this to be particularly true in Eastern Europe and India), operate their own PSPs; in more developed markets they are usually specialised services. If you intend taking payments from global customers, you may find a specialist more able to access the bewildering variety of payment schemes prevailing in different regions, although accessing them is one thing, delivering them effectively on your site checkout is another.

From a business case perspective, a reasonable default planning assumption prior to engaging in detailed negotiations with your banks and/or PSP, is that some combination of either fraud, increased CNP merchant fees, or fraud prevention services is likely to add around 1% of gross sales to your costs, in addition to PSP service/transactional costs themselves.

20.2.3 Accounting Policy

Some of the most thrilling days of my professional life have been spent with accountants, creating the T-diagrams for online retail operations. In brick-and-mortar retailing the stock movement out of the store, the payment by the customer, and the moment of recognising the sale are simultaneous at the point-of-sale. In online retailing, by contrast, there is almost always some sort of timing/phasing issue, which inevitably makes the standard double-entry book-keeping more intricate.

Some national accounting standards will prescribe the moment when an online sale can be recognised – typically the instant when the despatch of goods first takes place; otherwise a pure policy decision can be taken. Depending on your payment policy – on order, on despatch, on delivery (or collection) – then this is probably not simultaneous with the customer payment. Various messy accruals (especially across period boundaries) and reconciliation challenges need to be addressed. The messiness is increased if you are obliged to run two payment policies, for example card payments but also cash-payment on delivery, and/or if orders can be split across multiple deliveries. It isn't so much that these are especially difficult as that they are frequently inconsistent with the existing processes used in brick-and-mortar stores, and therefore require parallel accounting processes to be established.

20.3   Fulfilment

> *"Stocking, picking, packing, shipping,*
> *All without our standards slipping,"*
> sang Mary Poppins to the children, as she waited for the sweeps to
> collect another batch of parcels ready to drop down the chimneys of
> London.[90]

You may struggle to find this particular song in the original movie, but nevertheless these are the fundamental business processes of fulfilment. *Figure 52* describes it rather more professionally. (Click-

---

[90] OK, I made this one up

and-collect deserves a complete chapter to itself - **Chapter 26** - so it is out-of-scope for the purposes of this chapter.)

Figure 52 - fundamental fulfilment steps

I'll take a look at each in turn in the next sections, but first you should consider the option of outsourcing some or all of fulfilment. To start with, you are very likely to be outsourcing most of the shipping stage, although man-and-van delivery operations in metropolitan areas close to your stock location(s) are especially popular in China and Eastern Europe, with startling service levels (e.g. receive your order within 2 hours of placing it, for example). Many of the large shipping companies offer complete solutions, which may extend to customer service management, and which often also solve one of the nastier IT challenges too.

Aside from the pure economics of the business case for outsourcing, it has some other advantages. Despite the Mary Poppins ditty at the start of the section, the fulfilment cycle is much harder than it looks to perform consistently and reliably "without our standards slipping". Even a 2% failure rate in fulfilment can prove catastrophic to your overall business case, simply because errors are so costly to remedy. Take a look again at how many steps, and therefore potential staff time as well as direct costs, are involved in fixing the rather basic problem of the ripped party frock example I gave at the start of this chapter. Outsourcing can represent a significant de-risking of the whole project.

Where businesses re-introduce more risk instead of reducing it is when the fulfilment is partially outsourced, or outsourced to multiple third parties, without clearly defining the interfaces and boundaries. To the customer it looks like one process, which as far as they are concerned, you the retailer are performing. When a parcel arrives damaged, they are not interested in whether the goods were damaged in a warehouse or in a delivery van. Since you will have to remedy any failures, it is essential to tightly control the handover processes between each stage. For example the shipping company must agree that all the parcels it received from the packing stage for delivery were received in good condition, and that therefore any subsequent damage was their fault. This needs to be very tightly controlled in any contracts and standard operating procedures.

Perhaps the worst example I have seen is a retailer who outsourced warehousing (stocking and picking) to one third party, shipping to another, but then insisted on specifying, purchasing and designating the packing materials used themselves. They then economised by using substandard materials, and it cost them far more resolving endless disputes about liability for parcels arriving at customers with the goods in poor condition than they saved on materials (although to be honest I also think their shipping partner should have refused to accept such a contractual stipulation the first place).

20.4   Stock

The simplest and cheapest way to manage stock is to not have any.

Ensuring that the endless aisle does not require endless buying is often done by selling third party assortments through your website. When a customer places an order, you divert it to the third party. The difference from a marketplace-style offer, such as Amazon Marketplace, is that you are still deciding which products to list on your site and also that the customer is (usually) not aware that there is a third party involved. The extent to which you take ownership of the final shipping process to the customer varies. If you are working with a professional drop-ship vendor (DSV) who specialises in this business model — and these exist in many markets, including less mature markets (I've worked with one in Romania for example), especially in categories such as consumer electronics — then probably you will just hand-off this part of the order to the DSV, and expect order progress-status updates. On the other hand, if you are sourcing some specialist items from a cottage-industry supplier more focussed on quality-making-to-measure than on managing deliveries, you may prefer to handle the whole journey to the customer yourself. (There is also the question of branding the paperwork to consider – shipping notes, invoices etc – see below). Clearly the savings are not just less buying effort; it's also a way of avoiding stock risk on lower stock-turn items which are nevertheless necessary for a complete online range.

Otherwise you'll need some stock, and therefore a place to put it. At this point I suggest you re-read the available-to-promise chapter (**Chapter 16**). As a general rule, you will need a pool of stock which is isolated and dedicated to the online channel. That doesn't mean you aren't allowed to move stock in and out of this pool in a controlled way, but it does mean that it should not be "shared" in an uncontrolled way and subjected to channel conflict. The products which are fast-moving online are probably the same products which are fast-moving in brick-and-mortar, and shared stock pools will just generate too many situations where you are out-of-stock but your website doesn't realise this and keeps on selling the product.

Stock holding locations in brick-and-mortar retailing are usually stores and distribution centres (DCs). Using store shelf-stock is a recipe for out-of-stock situations as just defined. Using back-of-store stock usually *only* works if you ring-fence the website stock separately; it is a rare retailer which otherwise has such tight controls on back-of-store stock that it requires it to be booked in and out before moving it to the showroom floor. On the other hand properly ring-fenced back-of-store areas can be an excellent use of the space in under-performing stores! As soon as you try to employ more than one such store, however, the whole available-to-promise story can get a little more complicated – what if a customer orders two items, each of which is only in stock in different stores? It isn't unmanageable, but each small step in increased complexity needs to be taken carefully.

Using an existing DC presents a different challenge for most retailers. The first is that IT systems usually don't like it much. The second, much more important, is that DC operations for many retailers are simply not designed for the single-item picking processes required for customer order fulfilment; they are designed to optimise the bulk replenishment to stores, not fiddly picking and packing to customers. Breaking open supply chain shipping cases, for example, is not something you would do in bulk replenishment – it usually takes place when the goods are moved onto the store shelves – but is clearly mandatory for customer orders.

Therefore, the standard solution is another specialist warehousing operation, typically named a Fulfilment Centre (FC) to distinguish its operating model from a DC. That doesn't, of course, oblige it to be in a different physical location, but probably does oblige it to be treated almost as though it is (clients I have worked with who share the location refer to the separation of the DC from the FC as the "red line", regardless of whether one is really painted down the middle). Incidentally this specialisation of the FC operation away from the DC operation is another argument in favour of outsourcing until you have sufficient scale.

For business case planning assumption purposes, British Imperial measurements provide a particularly memorable rule-of-thumb: you can handle orders worth 1000 GBP per year per square foot of FC space[91]. In a more broadly useful metric measurement, this same rule-of-thumb translates roughly to the rather less memorable 13,450 EUR per year per square metre. Since sales density in practice is going to vary enormously depending on your assortment, then like all rules-of-thumb this one is only useful until you have the practical experience to ignore it (although it has actually proven surprisingly generally robust).

20.5   Picking

There are a couple of issues which might cause picking online orders to have somewhat different operating procedures and priorities compared to your existing processes. The first of these is specific, order level, service level agreement commitments to

---

[91] See for example data published by Asos.com, planning £1.2Bn of sales from 1M sq ft of warehouse. Amazon's 2011 10-K filing quotes $42Bn of product sales from 44M sq ft of warehouse, equating to around 600 GP per year per square foot, or roughly 8000 Euros per year per square metre; this probably reflects the relatively low price points of books and media, and may be slightly understated anyway as this space is referred to as "fulfilment and other" without giving any clues about the "and other".

customers, which are probably the main step-change from traditional mail-order. *Figure 53* shows the options currently offered by Amazon in the UK for example:

	Free Super Saver Delivery	One-Day Delivery	First Class (Standard Delivery)	Express Delivery	Evening Delivery	Expedited Delivery
Delivery Time	3 to 5 business days after despatch	One business day (including Saturdays) vafter dispatch	1 to 2 business days after dispatch	Orders before the Express deadline guaranteed to arrive by 1pm the next day	Orders before the Evening deadline guaranteed to arrive on the same day	Delivery times can vary from 1 to 3 days. Estimate shown in the order form

Figure 53 – Six delivery options offered by Amazon UK[92]

This section of the book is targeted at retailers starting out in online, to whom the best advice is… don't try this at home, especially options like "evening delivery". While six different classes of delivery service might be great customer differentiation, a single extra express option is more reasonable. An obvious, but related point, is not to over-promise, especially about order cut-off deadlines. "Order by 6pm for next day delivery" is a common type of promise, especially in the geographically compact countries of Europe. Remember all the steps that this involves, and especially the scheduled time when the courier will come and pick up your parcels which is an absolute cut-off (*Figure 54*). It's not going to be practical to make this particular promise if the courier arrives at 18:15 (unless you know a multi-drop van driver who is happy to hang around? I thought not).

Figure 54 - the long road to express delivery

The second issue is that generally it is worth prioritising accuracy at the expense of efficiency, especially if you are setting up this sort of operation for the first time, and this is often in contrast to how the rest of your logistics is set up. A 98% KPI might be very good for store

---

[92] From amazon.co.uk, December 2012

replenishment logistics, but it's dreadful for customer order fulfilment because of the high cost of each error. Typically this is addressed by picking-by-order even if the resulting picking-tours are not optimal, and by additional use of 4-eyes quality control processes. One retailer I worked with deliberately laid out its FC counter-intuitively, with the aim of ensuring that no two adjacent pick-faces had similar products in them, and thereby reducing the risk of accidentally picking a similar-looking but incorrect item.

20.6   Packing

The usual caveats about using planning rules-of-thumb are even more appropriate when budgeting for packing materials. Following the business-case theme of this section I feel obliged to quote a benchmark, so I suggest you start out targeting USD 1.50 per customer order. The quickest way to attack this figure is to purchase in bulk, but the quickest way to throw away some cash is to purchase in bulk before you have concrete experience of the way in which your customers order.

A typical, standard, non-food, B2C online operation, will have order sizes of somewhere between 1.5 and 2.5 items per order (although this often looks like 1,1,1,1,1,10 rather than 2,3,2,3,2,3 items). As far as possible you want to ship orders in as few deliveries as possible to keep costs down, but predicting in advance the "shape" of the packaging you might need is almost impossible. Start by buying a small number of various sizes of packets, and then see which ones you use the most of. I'd like to suggest a more scientific predictive approach, but practical experience is by far the best guide.

Whatever you do, don't economise excessively on materials quality. Similarly, don't economise on double checking the contents of those boxes before you seal them up for the shipper. Just keep remembering how much it's going to cost to remedy errors, never mind the reputational and brand damage. Just as an example, wine typically comes from the supplier in 6-bottle or 12-bottle cardboard cases. These are perfectly adequate when piled up into pallets, but are not really robust enough to just send as a parcel. *Figure 55* shows an example of protective repackaging (it's pretty heavy-duty cardboard too).

Figure 55 - re-packaging an online wine order

20.6.1 Printing

Every package will need to be accompanied by some form of documentation. There are six possible documents that most retailers need to consider: shipping note; invoice; returns form; shipping label; non-physical product documentation (especially extended warranties); marketing flyers and leaflets.

The shipping note is obvious – it says who from, who to, and what the package contains. What it usually does not do is mention prices and costs. The most practical reasons not to do so are twofold: a) it might be a gift; b) it is not ideal to tell anybody who might inspect the external documentation how much they would gain by stealing the contents. The second reason is nice, but doesn't take into account customs officials or pay-on-delivery processes. If cross-border shipping or payment on the doorstep are going to apply, then a paper invoice is mandatory (otherwise this is usually exclusively an email document in countries where fiscal printing is not anyway mandatory for tax reasons).

Clothing retailers include the documentation making returns easy, because this is a fundamental part of the proposition of selling clothing remotely. Other retailers, while not exactly obstructing returns, should consider at least making the customer put some effort into it. Provide the form on your website to be printed and completed by the customer, or possibly demand a call to your contact-centre first, especially if this gives you a chance to proactively intervene to prevent a return happening at all; anything to discourage gratuitous returns without preventing genuine ones.

All except the smallest man-and-van couriers will expect you to print the shipping label, usually machine readable, using software which they will typically provide, or at least to their specification. For any retailer big enough to have the courier collect, rather than themselves going to the post-office, some basic IT customisation to link shipping label numbers with your internal order numbers is usually worthwhile to make subsequent customer service simpler.

Warranty documentation is often sent separately by post, but of course you have to put the separate processes in place to do this. Occasionally this might also involve notifying the third-party providing the warranty at the same time.

Marketing material such as paper flyers are an obvious thing to do, and in fact can serve as a secondary revenue source if you can find partners who are interested in contacting your customers and don't represent any competition.

20.7   Shipping

Shipping is a two stage process: moving the goods from point A to point B; possibly then doing something at point B. Taking the "moving" part first, this is generally pretty straight forwards, until you start dealing with large items. Depending on exact health and safety regime you have to operate within, somewhere between 20Kg and 30Kg there will be a limit that says this is no longer a parcel that can be shipped by parcel-post. Equally even a lighter item, such as a very good racing bike or an aluminium ladder, will fall outside limits on awkwardly shaped packages. There are various ways these limits are defined by different carriers, but in general any single dimension larger than about one metre is going to prove challenging.

If you sell furniture, large electrical items, or very large quantities of commodity products (e.g. printer paper), you may find you need either a large item specialist service (the jargon is usually "2-man" service) or a pallet-shipper. The downside of such services is the cost of delivery, typically in the 30-40 Euro range in a compact European country, and potentially an awful lot more if you want to ship from say Sydney to Perth, or Moscow to Vladivostok. Even in a world of subsidising delivery out of marketing costs, some items may become completely uneconomic; typically these are bulky products with low margins – you won't find many online retailers who sell coffee tables for example, because these exactly fall between small=reasonable shipping costs and large=profitable enough to share shipping costs with the customer.

The upside of these carriers, especially a "2 man" specialist, is that they often offer a wide portfolio of possible premium services, which customers will be willing to pay extra for: delivery to room of choice, morning/afternoon/evening options, WEEE (old product) disposal, gas-fitting, plumbing-in, TV-set up. Their business model – in which a failed delivery because the customer was not available is an extremely expensive issue – tends to naturally promote premium service. Calling ahead, multiple SMS messages reminding the customer about delivery all feel like excellent service even though their primary objective is actually to keep costs down.

This leads naturally to the "possibly doing something at point B" side of shipping. Payment-on-delivery is the most obvious such something, either by cash or credit-card depending on the local prevailing consumer preference. But proof-of-delivery, delivery to room of choice, morning/afternoon options and so on, all offer possibilities for premium service (and fees) without significant additional cost. Furthermore there may possibly be local legal issues to contend with, such as ensuring that an adult signs for the receipt of products containing alcohol (restricted products vary bizarrely from country to country).

In summary, don't overlook the opportunities to make shipping into more than just delivering parcels. It can become an inherent part of your proposition and differentiation, without this necessarily driving excessive cost. However do plan ahead for the consequences, especially if you are proposing to sell "2 man" products. A customer who creates a perfectly reasonable seeming order such as a photocopier with an extended warranty and installation, some paper, and an ink cartridge for it, all in the same shopping cart, may well find themselves receiving four separate shipments, each handled by a different specialist shipping company (photocopier + installation = 2-man, paper= pallet-shipment, ink=standard parcel delivery, warranty=postal service). This has implications not just about cost, but about the whole order lifecycle – what happens if the ink gets spilled but the rest of the order arrives OK? Do you need four separate sets of paperwork, four partial invoices, four different payments collected on the door-step? Is the installation service a "product" as far as your IT and finance systems are concerned? How will you explain all this during the website checkout?

20.8   Issues and Returns

One aspect of retailing where you will be truly multichannel right from day one is handling returns and refunds. Even if your intention is to keep your brick-and-mortar and online channels as mostly separate propositions and operations to start with, customers will bring returns to your stores. It is impossible to prevent this (without major brand damage) by creating determined policies requiring online orders to be returned via online process – customers will still bring online issue to stores, where they can be sure of dealing with a person they can pin down and not an evasive email.

A lot can go wrong between an order being checked out and the customer receiving it satisfactorily. While returns may seem like a tedious side issue, returns rates even when your service is good can be quite high. As usual, I offer some benchmark planning figures with the warning that reality might be very different (*Figure 56*).

Category	Business Case Planning rule-of-thumb Returns Rate
B2C Food	<1%
B2C Wine	Approx 1.5%
B2C General Merchandise	Budget for 8%, probably a bit less if you are small
Consumer Electronics	Budget for 9-10%
Clothing	Budget for 30%

Figure 56 - benchmark planning returns rates[93]

In almost all categories the returns rate will increase as the price-point of the items increases. The highest reported figure I have heard was for a website selling very expensive shoes. Being both (broadly) in the clothing category and having a high price point, the returns rate reached a spectacular 85% without this actually being indicative of any real issues. Clearly such a business is only sustainable if you have gross margins to match! By contrast, cheap plain white T-shirts have negligible returns rates.

Customer expectations of returns policies vary widely by country, and especially by the strength of consumer protection legislation, and so it is impossible to define best-practice. Worst-practice is easier to define: defining your returns policy *after* selecting your third-party fulfilment partners, *after* briefing your IT teams, or *before* talking to your brick-and-mortar store managers.

20.8.1 Standard Issues List

What follows is a starting-point list of typical issues, for which I suggest that you should have a pre-defined documented process in place. There is no country I am aware of where it is acceptable to take the money and then not deliver the goods, so this is an obvious

---

[93] Reliable public domain data is very difficult to source, but see for example http://www.e-commercefacts.com/background/2011/08/10-tipps-to-reduce-return/

starting point. Inevitably there will be a thousand-and-one edge-cases, strange exceptions, and obstreperous customers which you cannot possibly pre-define, but it's always easier to improvise from solidly built foundations. Remember that many issues will involve a problem with a single product in a multi-product order. Incidentally, the key to writing basic procedures for these kinds of "infinite possibilities" situations is always to <u>write them assuming that only one thing goes wrong at once</u>.

Pick Fail: Failure to pick the complete order, due to stock issues

Missing Goods: Goods which the customer claims are missing a) when there is no proof they received them; b) when it would appear that someone else received them (this is particular important if you are operating pay-on-order or pay-on-despatch policies)

Damaged property: Customer's property damaged during the delivery, even though the goods themselves are fine

Unacceptably damaged goods: Goods delivered damaged. NB, many retailers have a "secret" threshold, typically around the $30 level, below which they judge it is cheaper to just send the same goods again for free without requiring a corresponding return, rather than manage a whole returns process

Acceptably damaged goods: Goods delivered damaged, but in a condition which the customer will accept if given a discount (for example a scratch on the side of an oven, which will be hidden from view when fitted in the kitchen)

Serial Offenders: Spotting serial offenders (customers whose orders apparently always have some sort of issue...)

Notified Returns: Returns notified by the customer; what process should they follow to get the goods back to you, where should they send them, what documentation is required?

Returned to store: Ordered online returned to store processes, especially for products not normally included in that store's assortment

Returns QA: QA process on receiving a return (ensuring that the box contains a faulty laptop, not a faulty brick)

Refund: Refund process. In many situations/countries there is a requirement that the return is issued to the same tender as the payment was made on because of a) credit card scheme rules; b) money laundering legislation

Unexpected returns: Un-notified returns (a box with some documentation just arrives spontaneously in the post)

Discretionary returns: Discretionary returns allowed ("I just didn't like it")? This is probably mandatory for clothing.

DSV returns: Returns to drop-ship vendors

Overseas returns: Returns from orders shipped overseas

20.9   Customer contacts and customer service

It is usual to measure customer contacts as a ratio of contacts-per-order. A contact is any message from the customer, including emails, phone calls, click-to-chat, webforms and certain kinds of social network actions (those which imply an action is required) especially twitter used as a more public version email. There is of course a decision to take about what contact channels you will make available to customers. There is a tradition for online pureplays to avoid publishing telephone numbers to keep costs down – not so long ago it was almost impossible to call Amazon for example. The business case for this has to be set against the long-term reputational issues caused by very disgruntled customers and more directly the short-term issue of lost sales because the customer is just not confident to order from such a site. "No phone number" sites are decreasing, which suggests that this business case is tipping in favour of better customer service preferred to lower costs.

An excessive contacts-per-order ratio is a key reason for an online store to become unprofitable, as they are often disproportionately expensive to address. Customer contacts occur for one of three basic reasons:

Pre-sales, for information. Some are unavoidable, but a high rate (> 0.1 / order for a typical business) can be a sign of insufficient information on your sites or, dare I say it, poor quality product data;

Pre-sales, for ordering. In markets where customers typically may not have access to online payment methods such as credit cards, and therefore pay by offline processes such as funds transfer from a bank, a website can become a sort of online catalogue in support of what is really a telesales operation. This model is particularly common in countries such as Russia where internet literacy is quite high but payment infrastructure is still developing. If you are in such a market, or if you decide that telesales are part of your business model anyway (there is only a small difference, so if you are building the infrastructure for eCommerce you may well want to consider adding telesales to it), then clearly such calls are probably a "good thing", and certainly should not be "counted" towards the contacts-per-order ratio ("bad thing");

Post-sales, due to some sort of order lifecycle issue. Universally these are a "bad thing".

The key to a successful customer-contact process is to ensure that the *agent handling the issue has at least the same information available as the customer does*. For example, if handling a pre-sales issue, the agent should be able to see the same website as the customer. If handling a post-sales issue, the agent should have timely information regarding the progress of all the items in the order, the financial/payment status etc.

For business-case planning purpose a benchmark is needed. Such data is extremely difficult to source in the public domain, so for this benchmark I am obliged to quote numbers from experience without really backing them up with representative quoted data. Counting only pre-sales for information plus post-sales for issues reasons (i.e. excluding "good" contacts for placing orders) combined, then *Figure 57* shows some reasonable numbers:

Contacts per Order	Applicable situations
0.2	About as good as it gets
1.0	What you can expect directly after launching
0.5 to 0.6	Where you should aim for 6-12 months after launch
Over 2.0	A major problem, stop focussing on driving sales and focus on fixing the process issues before your brand is ruined!

Figure 57 - Contacts per Order Benchmarks

If you are operating in a market where "good" pre-sales calls are the norm, then it is interesting to compare with eBay, who anecdotally have contacts-per-order ratios heading towards a grim-sounding 5.0 / order, the vast majority of which are pre-sales contacts, but allegedly have lower post-sales contacts rates, and more importantly much lower returns rates as a result. A variation on the same theme – providing information up-front reduces post-sales dissatisfaction - is that items with large numbers of customer reviews tend to have lower contact rates overall, another argument in favour of including ratings and reviews.

20.10 Top Takeaways

Order lifecycle includes the closely coupled topics of payment, warehousing, pick-pack-ship, returns, customer-services, some financial system tracking.

20.10.1 Payment, PSPs, Fraud, Accounting

Payment policies can be: pay-on-order, pay-on-despatch, pay-on-delivery. The choice of payment policy can have a major impact on order lifecycle. Payment is a two stage process: authorisation followed by capture.

Ensure you are familiar with local payment method processes, distance selling regulations, PCI/DSS compliance implications before selecting a payment policy.

Card/Customer Not Present (CNP) transactions are more expensive than face-to-face transactions. The costs rise when fraud prevention measures are inadequate. A budget of 1% of sales value should be allowed for either fraud costs or fraud prevention.

Payment Service Providers (PSP)/Payment Gateways process non-cash payment methods. PSPs may also include fraud prevention services. In many countries PSPs are operated by banks, but independent gateways exist in more developed online markets.

Accounting for online sales is different from store sales, because of the non-simultaneity of movement of cash and goods.

20.10.2 Stocking, picking, packing, shipping

Drop ship vendors (DSVs) exist in many markets, and can be used to operate stock-less models, especially in support of endless aisles.

Stocked models should usually ensure that stock is ring-fenced, consistent with the intended available-to-promise.

The operating model of a Fulfilment Centre (FC) is different from a traditionally store replenishment Distribution Centre (DC). Even if the two are co-located a "red-line" approach is recommended, to ring-fence stock and permit alternative operating procedures.

A benchmark rule-of-thumb for sizing a Fulfilment Centre is £1000 of orders per square foot per annum (=13450 Euro per square metre).

Fulfilment is very sensitive to error; errors are relatively very expensive to correct. Fulfilment Centre processes therefore emphasise accuracy at the expense of efficiency.

Multiple delivery options, especially express delivery to SLA cut-offs, require special processes. The cycle - place order, send to FC, print pick note, pick order , 4-eyes check, pack, label for courier, collected by courier – requires sufficient time to complete after the cut-off.

A rule-of-thumb benchmark planning figure for packing materials is $1.50 per order. Packaging needs to be robust enough to survive the stresses of the journey.

There are six possible documents that most online retailers need to consider: shipping note; invoice; returns form; shipping label; non-physical product documentation (especially extended warranties); marketing flyers and leaflets.

Oversized or heavy goods will require specialist shippers: pallet delivery or 2-man delivery. The cost of such services is much higher than parcel shipment. However they frequently offer the opportunity for additional differentiating services such as room-of-choice, installation/setup, old-item disposal.

Plan for orders which might require split shipment - such as the example of a photocopier plus pallet of paper plus ink cartridge plus warranty - and consider the impact on website checkout.

20.10.3 Returns and refunds

Returns will be multichannel from day one. Returns to store should not be resisted or refused. They could include items not normally ranged at that store.

Benchmark planning rates include 8% on general merchandise and 30% on clothing. Returns-rates increase with price-point.

Pre-plan returns policy for one level of issue per order (only): pick fail, missing goods, damaged property, unacceptably damaged goods, acceptably damaged goods, serial offenders, notified returns, returns to store, unexpected returns, QA, refunds, discretionary returns, DSV returns, overseas returns.

Returns and refunds issues may affect only a single item in a multi-item order.

Refund policy must take into account payment scheme rules and money laundering regulations.

Customer contacts occur for three main reasons: pre-sales for information, pre-sales for order, post-sales due to order lifecycle issues.

Customer contacts-per-order is a key measure of inefficiency. A distinction should be made between good contacts (offering sales opportunities) and bad contacts (due to bad product information or order lifecycle issues). Steady state rates should be between 0.2 and 0.6.

Chapter 21. I.T.

21.1 Introduction

Condensing complex topics like SEO or eMail marketing for retail, about which there are already shelves of books, into brief chapters is challenging. Condensing the entire libraries of material about I.T. for online retail is trebly so. (I should perhaps also confess at this point that I.T. was my first career, and I still derive a proportion of my consulting income from I.T. related work such as project design, high level business requirements, enterprise architecture, or vendor selection.)

Firstly a reminder of the scope of this part of the book: going online. Broader multichannel integration issues are therefore <u>excluded</u> from this chapter. Also deliberately excluded is any attempt to compare particular I.T. products or their suppliers. The eCommerce forums on the internet are full of questions of the "is software product X better than software product Y" type; this is the wrong question anyway. So what is the right question?

21.1.1 All the same

I'll start with a deliberately provocative assertion: all online retail stores are exactly the same. This is not quite yet true of mobile retail, where the conventions and best-practice standards have still to settle down, but is very much true of websites aimed at PCs. They all do the same few things:

Help: Help and information, and information functions (such as store locators);

My Account: Some sort of "my account" functionality, from the very basic where-is-my-order (known as WISMO) up to the quite sophisticated online wallets, personal preferences etc;

Home: A home page;

Category pages: A series of intermediate taxonomy pages i.e. the home pages for categories and sub-categories, special or seasonal offers etc;

Search: a search box, and search results pages;

Navigation: Various navigational filters which apply to the taxonomy pages or search results to help the customer drill down to the product he/she actually wants;

Product pages: Product pages themselves, including all the merchandising extras that go with them such as cross-sells, ratings, recommendations etc;

Basket: Shopping cart;

Checkout: Checkout, which normally has sub-steps asking who you are, how you want the goods delivered, where you want them sent to, and how you want to pay.

Behind the scenes are a number of key components supporting the online business, which again are almost the same at all retailers. The main differences in these parts of the ecosystem usually occur deep into the "back end integration" of the systems, and depend on the way in which the management of Order Lifecycle is coupled into existing systems, especially if you operate some sort of ERP.

21.1.2 All different

Where solutions do differ is firstly in their scalability. Amazon took 17 million orders during their peak 24 hour period in 2011[94]. A spreadsheet solution for order management probably wouldn't hack it for them. Secondly, in the depth of the functionality they offer. For example search or navigation can be very sophisticated, including features such as personalising the results to the customer, or dynamically tuning the search results to prioritise products which are proven to lead to better conversion. However, these sophisticated

---

[94] See for example http://www.ibtimes.com/inside-amazon-warehouse-photos-909410

features need sophisticated teams to manage them; they always require complex set-up and continuous ongoing tuning and monitoring. It is impossible to become Amazon on the day that you launch, and retailers who try to leapfrog over five years learning in five weeks tend to come a cropper. Of course there is no need to work it all out from scratch as the pioneering online retailers did, but a first class fully functioning I.T. ecosystem with all the processes and skills in place to support it is not something you can magic into being.

The third factor where there are some genuine differences between solutions are if your basic building blocks of retail – customers, products or prices – are unusually complex in some way and don't fit a standard B2C model. If any of the following considerations apply to your retail business model, then get these on the table up-front in any discussions with software solutions or suppliers:

Complex customers: If there are any relationships or restrictions between two separate customers (this is usually only applicable to B2B, where one logon might be allowed to build a cart, but only the supervisor logon can checkout);

Complex pricing: If your pricing is not a one-price-fits-all model at SKU level i.e. there is not always a single "current price" for a given SKU which does not vary with the purchase volume or (especially) the identity of the customer;

Complex promotions: If you absolutely *must* have promotional structures where the existence of one product in a cart can affect the price of another (e.g. buy two shirts and get a free neck-tie). If you study most leading online sites you will find that they tend to avoid promotional pricing structures like link-saves, multi-saves, multi-buys and so on – these structures are awkward to handle in an online environment. Many retailers who operate these offers in store do not replicate them online, and in fact a trend partly driven by multichannel is to reduce the complexity of promotional structures in general, to keep promotions consistent across channels;

Complex products: If you have any of the following "complex" types of product:

1. Items with variants (e.g. colours or sizes). Most solutions will handle these OK, but check there are no limits like only one dimension (i.e. colour but not size simultaneously)

2. Loose-weight (e.g. screws or nails) or catch-weight (e.g. chickens) products where the item is priced per Kg not per unit

3. Any items where the calculation of ATP will be difficult (e.g. two three metre ropes do not make a six metre rope)

4. Any items which are not added to cart in whole numbers (e.g. 1.2 metres of rope)

5. Non-physical products (e.g. warranties). Most solutions will be OK, but double check

6. Configurable items like PCs (or BMWs!), where the customer could add different features

7. Any products where a single item in a cart could generate multiple lines on an invoice (e.g. a dining table + chairs)

8. Listings i.e. where the same SKU from two different suppliers are two different products

9. Almost anything else where a simple model 'one item added to cart = one item to pick in the warehouse = one item to ship = one line on an invoice' is not appropriate

10. Products which require specialist shipping (i.e. anything that won't fit in a small parcel).

21.1.3 Archetypal architecture

Without further ado, here is a (very!) high level overview diagram of an archetypal online retail I.T. ecosystem (*Figure 58*):

Figure 58 - I.T. ecosystem archetype

Quickly getting the acronyms and abbreviations out of the way:

CRM: customer relationship management;

OMS: order management system;

ATP: available to promise;

WMS: warehouse management system;

ERP: enterprise resource planning (system);

Rich Media: digital asset management – managing pictures and videos, often a separate system for high volume sites primarily for performance reasons;

Analytics: will be described below;

Tax & Ship: only necessary in certain countries (such as the US), external services for the calculation of sales taxes and shipping rates;

Credit: or any other special payment arrangements such as accounts, subscriptions etc;

Ratings: shorthand for Ratings & Reviews.

At its most simplistic, if you can firstly tick all these boxes, and then secondly tick integrating the boxes together, then you have all systems go. The fundamental difference between a billion dollar website and a kitchen-table web-store is that the big player will tend to have high-performance, full-featured, specialist products doing each of these jobs while the small player might well have a single generic package supplemented by a few spreadsheets; even the smallest players might still use some specialist components (for analytics for example).

Standard components are cheap. Specialist components are expensive (I'm sure any IT managers reading this will identify with the experience of shuddering when a vendor announces that theirs is an "enterprise class solution" – a euphemism for adding a couple of extra zeros to the price tag). Getting components to work by themselves is straightforward (i.e. cheap). Integrating different components together is difficult, and therefore expensive.

21.2   Choosing solutions

I asserted in the introduction to this chapter that forum questions like "is software product X better than software product Y" are the wrong question. This class of questions are typically posted on online forums by small-medium retailers trying to wade through a jargon ridden and technology-biased swamp, and it is to them that this section is particularly aimed.

Online retail I.T. differs in two extremely helpful ways from other I.T. Firstly, all retail websites genuinely do perform broadly the same functions. Secondly they are all on view in public, unlike say a back-office finance system or warehouse management system, where you are unlikely to be able to view the functionality details of large numbers on a daily basis. You can quickly gain insight even into the less visible parts on an online retail solution by ordering something from the site and then returning what you ordered. (Professionally I have to look at large numbers of websites, and I always start by reading the delivery options and returns pages, and then experimenting with the checkout, which together tell me far more about how the business works than browsing the assortment might.)

A "classic" I.T. selection process will consists of making a very detailed list of all the things you need the solution to do, and then inviting suppliers to tick the items in the list. The trouble with this approach for something as standard as online retail is that you will end up with everybody ticking 97 out of 100 boxes. This is just as true for the very top-end systems as it is for the most basic ones – as soon as you are comparing solutions in the same "class", it's like comparing Coke with Pepsi. However this idea of "class" does give a good starting point. I.T. solutions can be divided into the following (extremely broad) clusters (*Figure 59*):

	High Level Delivery Approach	
	Software packages which need to be "installed" by someone	Cloud / SaaS (software as a service) / Hosted
Target Solution Tier		
Only for the biggest players	Large scale frameworks, intended to be integrated with lots of specialist components	
For 2nd or 3rd generation larger websites	Fairly complete packages, with a good number of well-defined integration points	"Complete" solutions with globally applicable functionality
Small-medium retailer or 1st generation websites	As above, but usually without the scalability or integration flexibility	Fairly complete solutions but usually only applicable in single countries and for the more standard types of products
Very Small	"OK, now install the CD-ROM" packages	In many countries 1001 "online cart" options, often provided by generic web players (such as the search engines)
Kitchen-table	Freeware	C2C Marketplaces

Figure 59 - IT solution classes

So what? Now is a good moment to go back to the "all different" subsection just above. It isn't an accident that Amazon started with books, or that if you look at all but the most developed multichannel markets many or most of the top online stores are all in media or consumer electronics.[95] These are very "standard" online categories i.e. simple. The right place to start when selecting solutions is to ask "how is my business model, differentiation, proposition or operating model different from just being a vanilla online book-store?" (Don't picture Amazon, picture a plain basic store!). If the answer to this question is "not much if at all", then head towards the right-hand column at a scale that fits your budget and ambitions. If the answer is "a lot" then aim left and higher. If you are larger retailer reading this section anyway despite its introduction, then at this point the Forrester Waves, Gartner Quadrants et al are a good idea.

The next step is to always *simultaneously* choose software and implementation partner (even if this partner is your own I.T. department, or just yourself if you are a very small start-up). <u>Never</u> pick one and then the other ("I want someone who can implement package X", "Z are good, let's get them to implement package X"). Package X is not better than package Y, live business solution X is better than live business solution Y. If you force a good implementation partner to use unfamiliar technology, or give a good package to a bad partner, you will most likely end up with business solution which is poor, expensive or late; a few minor extra features will be no compensation.

Then focus again on those *differences* from the standard book-store; they are where 80% of the challenge in the project will be. If at all possible (i.e. unless you have created something quite unique), do not be the first to do this specific functionality with this partner with this software. Insist on talking to someone else who has already been there, and don't focus on the standard/easy 80% of the functionality - every retail website has product pages. And insist that your partner demonstrates how it proposes to tackle these specific differences.

Define any expected integrations with existing systems you may already have. Focussing again on the differences from the book-store, are there any places where you will need to integrate some

---

[95] See for example internet retailer top 300 Europe guide

specialised, or best-in-class, bits of software? Integration is the most difficult part of I.T.

Finally, never sign a contract until you have done a workshop to design how the checkout is going to work. Don't get excited (yet!) by things like beautiful artwork depicting your home-page design. Sitting down and working through the checkout process will tell you whether your partner and software is going to be able to do the job, because a) it will force you to consider almost all the difficult details of your proposition and b) it will tell you if you and your partner can communicate. All I.T. projects discover small surprises along the way; the trick is to try and avoid large surprises which completely invalidate half the work already built.

21.3 Key components

In the next few sub-sections, we'll take a brief look at a few of the key components listed in *Figure 58*. Many of them have in effect already been covered elsewhere, so for example I'm not intending to talk *again* about product data from a peculiarly I.T. perspective. Some are indicative of integrations back into existing areas of your I.T. (for example a CRM system or Finance system), and so again won't be covered. Some, like WMS or Payment Gateway, are generic solutions anyway, and their requirements have already been covered previously; a WMS solution for online retail is not, apart from what has been discussed in *Chapter 20*, so different from any other WMS.

21.4 Site Design

Once again, I'm going to take you back to Moscow 1960, only this time with a slight change from the previously presented *Figure 9*.

Figure 60 - Moscow 1960 bishops on offer

Figure 60 is the same chess position, but with a bit of promotional hype. And I can now guarantee that those same experienced chess-players who could digest and recognise this whole position in less than one second will be completely unable to perform that feat now the layout has been mucked around slightly, despite exactly the same data being on display. The same logic extends to website design. All good online retail websites look pretty much the same and do pretty much the same things. This is not lack of imagination on the part of retailers, nor is it imposed by limitations of their I.T. systems. It is because customers *need* to be able to rapidly digest the information presented. If they can't, they don't spend time being intrigued by the fascinating new design paradigm, instead they quickly switch to someone offering a more familiar pattern.

A whole set of conventions has emerged through trial and error, best-practice is quite easy (if lengthy) to describe, and customers are turned off not just by poor design but by unfamiliar design. This is just beginning to happen for mobile sites (of which more later in **Chapter 25**). Compare for example these three top-level navigation screens from three different European countries (**Figure 61**):

Figure 61 - 3 countries, 3 mobile navigation screens[96]

These are top retail sites in their respective different countries and yet are remarkably similar when you think how many different ways there could be to lay out navigation. In this area, at least, mobile is headed the way of the good old PC – to standardisation of the user interface experience. In fact if you have a read of the technical documentation for developing Android applications, theoretically an open platform where imagination could rule, in fact a great deal of it is focussed on standardisation of the user interface.

That isn't to say that there are not cultural differences, but they tend to be common across the entire culture, and to exist for a well-proven and founded reason. Take a quick look at a Chinese eCommerce site, for example, and you will typically be confronted by a wall of text; a designer familiar only with western design patterns will be able to explain at length to you why this is not best practice and how it will put consumers off. But Chinese is a relatively slow language to type in, and so the home-page typically has to perform the duties that a search box would perform on an alphabetic language

---

[96] Collage from bol.com Netherlands, otto.de Germany, Tesco direct UK

site. Chinese consumers want to click a mouse on a link, not painfully type into a box, and so navigational links tend to predominate in the use of space. Best practice is different, but best practice and consumer familiarity are still fundamental.

Much as I might enjoy writing such a text, this book cannot possibly be a comprehensive guide to retail website design (maybe the next book if this one sells well!); the screenshots required alone would double its size, let alone the commentary. I will therefore confine myself to the following top ten tips:

21.4.1 Fast response times

Find out what is the slowest connection bandwidth that covers 90-95% of your target customers. If the majority will connect via GSM-mobile links, or via 56K dial-up modem – and this is still true in many regions – then design your website for them; lots of high quality images or video might look beautiful over the fast link in your offices, but will take a few hours to load over GSM. "Broadband" is a variable concept too, so state a precisely-defined benchmark connection speed and make sure all your pages load on that connection in less than 2 seconds.

There are some well-publicised statistics about page-loading times and their impact on sales/conversion rates. One of those "source of the Amazon" quotes which is widely touted but the original seems to be lost in myth is that each 0.1s (100 milliseconds) extra delay in loading pages costs 1% of sales.[97] A better founded, and more recent, data-point suggests that a one second extension in page-load times results in 7% lower conversion[98]. It's that old favourite One Second Rule again in a slightly different form.

---

[97] Amusingly this statistic is even quoted in academic papers, for example this one –
http://wwwdb.inf.tu-dresden.de/misc/team/boehm/pubs/diss_final.pdf   -
but the very formally quoted source then turns out to be someone's blog with (yet another) anecdotal reference in it!
[98] http://www.aberdeen.com/Aberdeen-Library/5136/RA-performance-web-application.aspx

21.4.2 No roadblocks or locked doors

Never *require* your customers to log in or register in order to checkout (or worse still, browse). Always have a guest checkout option. In general, never make any "extra" data *mandatory* over-and-above the minimum needed to successfully complete the transaction. The temptation to capture extra for re-marketing purposes later may be strong but making it compulsory should be resisted; there's no harm in optional requirements so long as it is very clear they are optional and the incentives for doing so are plain (e.g. loyalty points). There is a famous and oft quoted example: "the 300 million dollar button", in which simply removing the requirement to register during checkout generated $300M of extra sales for the website in question (OK, it was already a big site).[99]

21.4.3 Make sure checkout is about checking out

Online checkout is a complicated process. Getting a customer to the end of it requires focussing them on the job at hand. Enclose the customer in it. Do not distract them with new offers half-way through (save them until after the customer has confirmed the order!), and do give them a progress overview (***Figure 62***) to encourage them on the journey when they start to ask "are we nearly there yet?"

Figure 62 - Checkout Progress Bar

21.4.4 No nasty surprises

The top reason for customers to abandon their shopping carts is "sticker shock" – finding out that their order is going to cost a whole lot more than they thought by the time they arrive at the order summary page. Give them the bad news up front. Sucking the customer into the transaction only to play them for a sucker at the end is for budget airlines. It says you are a "cheap" (in every sense of that word) brand.

---

[99] http://www.uie.com/articles/three_hund_million_button/

21.4.5 It's the products stupid

Every page on a retail website (except checkout!) is a product page. It should always be possible to add something directly to the shopping cart from every non-checkout page on a retail site.

True product pages should focus first on ensuring that the customer knows what they are buying if they choose *this* product, and only second on trying to sell them alternative or extra products.

21.4.6 It's the stupid customer

Every page should have a Call to Action: it must be possible to decide what to do next within one second, and the Call to Action should stand out on the page; remember the One Second Rule. It should not be necessary to read the page as though it is a mortgage contract before knowing what to do or where to click.

21.4.7 Below the fold is another county

80% of customers won't read any part of a web-page that requires them to scroll down. One of the more esoteric, although perfectly valid, disciplines that has developed significantly as a consequence of the web is eyeball-tracking; monitoring where on a page users are focussed, and then creating a heat-map indicating where user attention is most concentrated on average. I've drawn an artificial one in *Figure 63*.

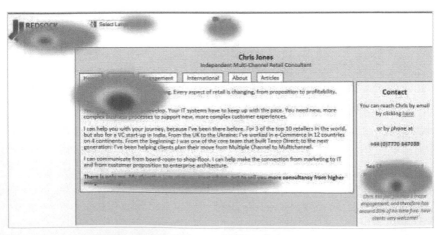

Figure 63 - web page heat map

One thing such maps show fairly clearly is that below the fold is foreign territory for the majority of customers. This does NOT mean you should cram the top part of every web-page full of as much information as possible; you will end up without clear Calls To Action, which is far more fatal. But it does mean that whenever your design agency brings you yet another "portrait layout" screen design, you should be ready with a ruler and a blank piece of card to place across it and see what it would look like if you only view the un-scrolled area.

21.4.8 Be conventional

As already discussed, there is a standard layout that customers expect for each language layout family (left-to-right alphabetic like English, right-to-left alphabetic like Arabic, Chinese, etc). An English language page should flow from top-left to bottom-right, have top navigation, left-filtering navigation, top-to-bottom forms flow etc. Don't break these conventions, they are the result of years of trial and error, and are now so familiar to customers that they are self-fulfilling.

21.4.9 Tell customers where to find or get help

FAQ and help pages are not an optional afterthought to be written in the 25 minutes before you finally go live. If you don't reassure your customers that it's all going to be OK if they risk giving their money to a screen instead of a human, then they won't.

21.4.10 Don't believe any of the previous nine tips

Online, there is no need to *believe* anything. You can *always* measure it. Guidelines like these top ten tips are nice, but only useful until you have some empirical data to replace them. In order to capture such data you will need an Analytics tool...

21.5 Analytics

On a <u>single channel</u> such as a retailer web-shop it is possible to monitor every customer through every page of their journey. Online you don't monitor them by name (usually, and especially not without permission!), but in aggregate. Usually most interesting are the transitions from one page to the next.

Analytics is built around the idea of measuring goals. The usual goal for a retailer is to get customers to checkout, and so a typical analytics report (funnel report) will look something like **Figure 64**.

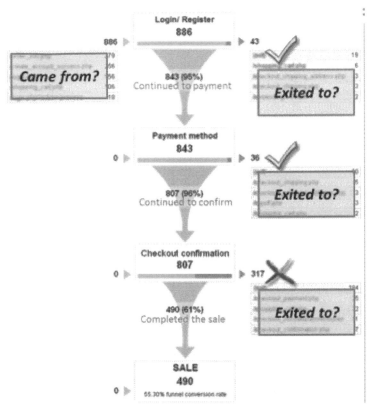

Figure 64 - analytics conversion funnel

In this example the retailer has a good checkout in terms of retaining customers through it, but then some sort of problem with the checkout confirmation screen – at a guess this is probably a case of sticker shock again! Being able to quickly spot this kind of issue, and then do something about it, is one areas where online retailing is much easier than brick-and-mortar.

A related use of analytics is for A/B-testing processes (or multivariate testing if you want to be an advanced user and change more than one thing at once). You try two different versions of something – say the special offer banner on the home page – and then measure which one is more effective in achieving your goals, be that checkouts or just visitors to the details of the offer. More sophisticated IT systems will let you do this testing simultaneously, by randomly serving up customers with the two different versions (typically in a 50/50 split for something like a new promotional graphic, or a 90/10 split for something scary like a new checkout process which might actually make things worse not better). Because you can often get statistically meaningful results in less than 24 hours, it's incredibly powerful despite its simplicity.

Failing to do all this is flying blind, like running a corner-store without ever watching your customers shopping in it. Since there are even freeware tools available (such as Google Analytics – as always no endorsement or otherwise implied), there is no excuse not to monitor website analytics. It's one of the absolute basic disciplines.

21.6   Order Management

Order Lifecycles, as discussed in **Chapter 20**, can be complex. The need for some sort of I.T. system to manage them depends largely on scale. If you are retailing from your kitchen table, and your order lifecycle process consists of picking and packing a dozen orders each morning and then taking them down to the local post-office, you can just keep track on a spreadsheet. If you are Amazon doing 17 million orders in a peak 24 hour period, then something a bit grander is going to be required. The difference between the most basic and the grandest includes (but is by no means limited to!) the following key factors. The first, scale, is obvious.

The second is the complexity of your orders. As soon as a single customer order can consist of more than one shipment, then complexity increases exponentially, especially if your order lifecycle might accompany split shipments with split payments. The underlying structure (of which this is only the tip of the iceberg) might start to look like **Figure 65**.

Figure 65 - order complexity, 2nd level

The third is whether or not an order management system is just essentially a database that records what has happened, such what the current status of each shipment is, or whether it can tell other systems (or people) to do things proactively at specific times or in response to specific situations e.g. "these 10 customers should expect their sofa to be delivered tomorrow, so we will now send them a delivery information SMS".

The fourth is a more subtle I.T. architecture design issue. Which system is "in charge" of what? This is particularly important if the order management system needs to be interfaced to a warehouse management system. Can the OMS tell the WMS what to do? Who is responsible for making sure that you don't have too many orders to fit in the shipping company's collection van today?

Fifthly, does the OMS take responsibility for coordinating available-to-promise? As soon as your promise gets even a little bit complicated – such as shipping the same product from two different locations – you need something to do this job. The OMS is a prime candidate because it also knows the status of each order, including things like whether a customer has just cancelled and therefore some stock has come free.

Once you move from thinking about only a single channel (i.e. the website that this part of the book is primarily about) into multiple channels, a reasonably sophisticated OMS solution is going to be mandatory. Even a single website solution usually has some sort of customer service function, and the customer-service operators need somewhere to be able to view – and amend – orders; this inevitably impacts on the OMS, and some OMS solutions include a customer-service capability either by default or as an optional extra.

21.7   Search & Merchandising

If there is one component where a bit of extra complexity will quite probably lead to a lot of extra sales it is search functionality. Most packages come with one in the box. Many are decidedly average. Experiment on a few mid-sized retailer websites if you don't believe me. Even very large retailers can make a bemusing job of it. My favourite example (I won't put the screenshots in here, read my blog if you want to find it[100]!) was a leading retailer running a promotion based around a charity link up, whose strap-line was a single "made up" word. I tried this word in their search box, and the top 3 results included a dictionary to help me with my spelling! Oh, and no reference to their charity link-up offer.

If you are at the "buying a solution" stage, have a serious discussion about whether a specialist component would be feasible. There are some good freeware solution possibilities, so this need not involve extra direct cost – although of course there will be integration requirements.

Search doesn't work well automatically – it has to be tuned/configured. There are search solutions which are self-tuning, but even these need a different kind of tuning, because they learn from experience (essentially they move the results customers most frequently click towards the top). Tuning search, in case you are wondering, means getting sensible, intuitively optimal, results to consistently appear at the top of the list of results, something which actually doesn't come terribly naturally to search systems(!). Include

---

[100]   http://www.redsockmultichannel.blogspot.co.uk/2012/06/fix-cross-functional-before-you-try-do.html

the lead-time to do this in your implementation plans, and remember that it can't be done until after your product data is mostly ready...

There is an armada of merchandising tools out there, all of which aim to do approximately the same thing: make it more likely that, out of your wide variety of products, you will display to your customers the ones they are most likely to actually want or buy. Many of the same comments apply as for search itself, and in fact there is increasingly a cross-over between the two, running under the banner of searchandising. They still need configuring, monitoring and tuning – there is no such thing as a free lunch. (The most sophisticated of all come under the banner of personalisation – the topic of **Chapter 24**.)

The same challenges also apply: integration at the implementation stage, and especially measuring the benefits at the operation stage. If you plan to implement any such tool, try to phase it into your plans at a time when your business is otherwise fairly static, so that it becomes easier to identify any overall cause-and-effect relationships. Often the improvements directly attributable to the tool will be offset by reductions elsewhere (e.g. a tool that drives customers towards best-sellers, but then negatively impacts the long tail; it might have overall positive benefit, but of a two-steps-forward-one-step-back kind.) Most tools are not immediately effective, either because it takes time to tune them, or even if they are mainly self-tuning, it takes time for them to learn.

21.8   Budget

Retailing is typically a rather thrifty sector when it comes to I.T. spending. Online, where the web-site is effectively occupying the budget-space that brick-and-mortar store estate would do, spending is relatively higher expressed as a percentage of turnover. **Figure 66** is an approximate synthesis of several reasonably consistent surveys[101].

---

[101] For example, see Forrester, State of Retailing Online 2009

Figure 66 - online retail I.T. spend

21.9 Top Takeaways

Online retail sites typically do a standard set of things: Help, My Account, Home & Category Pages, Search, Navigation, Product Pages, Cart, Checkout.

Variations from the standard set which typically might cause issues include: complex customers; complex pricing, especially customer-specific pricing; complex promotions which generate relationships between products and their prices; complex products, especially those which cause the calculation of ATP to be difficult, or which violate a simple model 'one item added to cart = one item to pick in the warehouse = one item to ship = one line on an invoice'

Advice for the small-medium player choosing IT solutions: focus on the differences from a vanilla book-store – the non-standard 20% will be 80% of the project effort; choose the supplier simultaneously with the software; clearly identify all expected inter-system integrations – integration is much harder than single system implementation; do a joint checkout design workshop *before* signing a contract.

Retail website design has adopted standard conventions. These are consistent within cultures. Break them at your peril.

Top considerations for site design: always remember the One Second Rule; page-load times consistent with expected customer bandwidth; no unnecessary mandatory logins/data; enclose the checkout; no nasty surprises; every page is a product page; clear calls to action; care below the fold; be conventional; provide help; never believe lists like this – test and measure instead.

Analytics is not optional. Everything online is measurable.

The need for a specialised Order Management System is determined by: scale; order complexity, especially split orders; co-ordination and proactivity in managing fulfilment; lead system; ATP coordination; multiple channels including customer-service.

Seriously consider a specialised search component, no matter what type or scale of solution you are otherwise implementing.

Search, merchandising, and searchandising tools all need time to be tuned or to self-tune.

I.T. spending as a percentage of sales is much higher online than for brick-and-mortar retail. It is a transfer of cost from store estate to technology. Benchmark planning figures are 2% offline, 7% online.

Chapter 22.   Organisation

22.1   Size

More than any other topic, organisational size is the one where retailers most want to know "what others retailers like us" are doing. Unfortunately, more than any other topic, this is an area that is particularly difficult to make comparisons. No two retailers are alike, and in fact no two job descriptions are alike.

Because the question invariably comes up, I have eventually developed a sort of ready-reckoner, designed to suggest the incremental headcount required by a brick-and-mortar retailer adding online channel(s). It assumes that the organisation required to run brick-and-mortar retail is already in place, and therefore is not appropriate to headcount sizing for an online pure-play; it strictly considers incremental headcount only. I've based it on real organisations I've either worked with or received information from, and then tested it with others to validate it. It has proven surprisingly robust give or take 20% or so in either direction, but I would strongly warn anybody against using it as anything more than a very rough guide.

It is designed to work as a small spreadsheet lookup table and formula, so it's a bit clumsy when put into print. First take a look a *Figure 67*.

	A	B	C
1	Sales Baseline, in millions of Euros	Base staff	Additional staff per million Euros of sales above baseline
2	0	2	0.6
3	10	8	0.4
4	20	12	0.3
5	30	15	0.3
6	40	18	0.2
7	50	20	0.16
8	100	28	0.12
9	200	40	0.067
10	500	60	0.04
11	1000	80	0.03
12	2000	110	0.015

Figure 67 - incremental head count ready reckoner

Fairly simply, you first find the highest row whose baseline online sales you will exceed. So suppose you will have online sales of EUR 35 million, you would locate row 5, the one with the baseline figure of 30 in column A it. It suggests base staff of 15 column B. Then for each one million EUR of sales above the baseline figure, add that number of staff from column C. So in this case, you have 35 − 30 = 5 million of sales above baseline, and therefore require 5 * 0.3 = 1.5 additional staff, for a total of 16.5 altogether.

22.2   Structure

A simple suggested outline structure for a small-medium "online" team within an existing brick-and-mortar retailer is shown in *Figure 68*.

Figure 68 - simple online organisation structure

Plainly such a team does not exist in a vacuum, and so ***Figure 69*** shows its key relationships within a wider generic retail organisation.

Figure 69 - extended organisation

We are here starting to walk a fine line towards a truly multichannel organisation, which is the subject of the next chapter, ***Chapter 23***. This chapter continues the consistent theme of this section of the book, which is going online in the first place, and therefore focusses on the starter "semi-detached" organisation that is typical at this stage of a retailer's multichannel development.

Although I have used the word "manager" in some of the boxes, "management" would perhaps by more appropriate: there is no implication here that these are single jobs for a single person, or even just a single tier in an organisation. What follows is an extremely brief outline description of each suggested function. Anything more specific needs a detailed understanding of your particular organisation and chosen set-up; every retailer is simply too different when it comes to job roles and organisation design to get into precise job specifications in a general handbook.

22.2.1 Marketing & Merchandising

This area is responsible for the proposition: user-experience, design of the website and other online channels, promotional activities and calendar, and probably also high level assortment design. Its most important task is not directly online at all, it is ensuring that the offline and online propositions are consistent. While this once again leads us towards multichannel considerations, in its more basic form it means ensuring that things like trading and promotional calendars are synchronised.

22.2.2 Web Marketing

There are a significant number of specialist technical competencies in marketing an online proposition, as outlined in *Chapter 18*, including SEO, SEM, email marketing and web analytics. These require one or more specialists to manage and deliver.

22.2.3 Webshop Management

Just like a brick-and-mortar store, an online store is constantly changing: New products and prices, new features and functionality, new systems and seasons. Processes need to be defined and managed, and everything needs to be continuously tested. There is often a constant stream of associated IT development activities that need to be coordinated with the business.

22.2.4 Data / Administration

You've read the chapters (**Chapter 15** and **Chapter 19**). Someone's got to do it. It might as well be you. See the next chapter for how to make sure it's someone else!

22.2.5 Operations & Fulfilment, and Customer Service

While a good proposition might generate sales, only a good fulfilment operation can keep costs down to a level where these sales are actually profitable. As suggested in the Order Lifecycle chapter (**Chapter 20**), this is typically sufficiently different from bulk activities supporting stores that new specialist roles are required.

22.3 KPIs

A consequence of everything online being so easily directly measurable is that almost every business process can have some sort of key performance indicator associated to it, and so you can end up wih a huge list. At a high level, I suggest the following two short lists as a starting place. Although the list is very short, it includes at least one KPI which measures the most critical objective of each contributing function. It also includes those KPIs which most easily maintain a healthy tension between functions. For example, gross demand could be easily enhanced by making impossible shipping promises, which would then adversely impact OTIF and probably delivered margin.

Firstly, monitoring marketing (Figure 70):

KPI	Description
Gross Demand	Total value of the order checked out on website
Acquisition cost	marketing spend per "new" (the definition varies) purchasing customer, or more simply per checkout. Typically this is broken down further via analytics to consider the different channels of marketing spend (did this checkout arrive via SEO, affiliate marketing etc)
Net Churn	New unique customers giving you enough information to market or re-market them effectively *minus* existing customers who have not recently visited

Figure 70 - website marketing KPIs

Secondly, monitoring trading (Figure 71):

KPI	Description
Net Sales	Value of orders net of returns and refunds (typically the equivalent target for buying)
Delivered margin	Gross margin + fees (delivery, services) – direct delivery/shipping costs
Conversion rate	% of website visitors who checkout

Figure 71 - website trading KPIs

Finally, monitoring the efficiency and effectiveness of the operation (*Figure 72*).

KPI	Description
Contacts per order	Ratio of customer contacts (phone, email, service desk in store, twitter etc) per order checked out
OTIF	On Time In Full. The % of checked out orders which were fully and successfully delivered to the customer within the published service levels
Assortment serviceability	The % of the published online assortment which is actually available for customers to purchase (usually measured at the start of the day).
Site availability	% of time that the site was fully functional for customers (this is often measured by an external "heartbeat monitoring" service, and/or in more sophisticated retailers by application performance management tools). It's best to try and measure this "externally" i.e. from the web, not from inside your own infrastructure.

Figure 72 - operational efficiency KPIs

22.4   Top Takeaways

Incremental organisational headcount can be loosely predicted, but every organisation is different.

Incremental tasks include: marketing & merchandising, online marketing, webshop management, data administration, fulfilment, customer-service.

Key KPIs for measuring marketing: gross demand, acquisition cost, customer churn.

Key KPIs for measuring trading: net sales, delivered margin, conversion rate.

Key KPIs for measuring operations: contacts-per-order, OTIF, assortment serviceability, site availability.

Part D – From Multiple Channel to Multichannel

Chapter 23.   Multichannel Organisation

23.1   Introduction

The organisation described in the previous chapter is nice, but it isn't multichannel. It is probably the most appropriate approach for a retailer newly going online, and which temporarily needs a ring-fenced organisation in order to get started and build up some momentum. It is surprising, however, how many retailers still equate being multichannel with having a website, or even make statements such as "we have stores and we have multichannel", as though stores were in some way not part of being multichannel.

Your customers certainly won't see it that way. As already discussed in the introduction (*Chapter 1*), they expect you to be present on all the channels they want to use and will penalise you if you are not. Trust is an essential element of any online channel (and of retail in general of course), and if your channels are inconsistent, they are untrustworthy. If you go one step further and start implementing self-evidently multichannel customer journeys such as click-and-collect, then inconsistency is not just untrustworthy, it is unacceptable.

Figure 7 illustrated a typical multichannel shopping journey: there are 14 touch-points in this journey, spread across six channels. *Figure 73* takes this to its logical organisational conclusion: although each of the touch-points has a different role in the overall customer experience, you want a consistent journey for a consistent brand, and the best way to deliver that is by consistent organisation in a consistent retailer.

Figure 73 - omni-channel shopping, many channels but one experience

This is the kind of thing that it's easy for a consultant to write on a slide, but in reality it represents a huge change management challenge that most retailers prefer to defer until their online channel is at least well established and proven to be generating sales.

23.2   The 4-stage organisational model

Not only is it preferable to phase in the challenge of organisational change, but in practice it would almost certainly be suicidally disruptive to try and get there in one single jump from camp zero. Four archetypal organisational stages characterise the transition (**Figure 74**); what is important is not awareness of such a model but having a conscious plan. Don't let any organisational cracks start to become visible to customers as disjointed gaps in their experience.

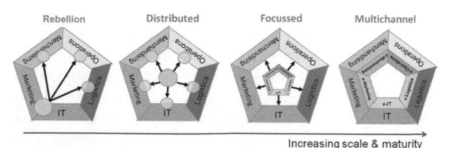

Figure 74 - four-stage multichannel organisational maturity model

I'd like to say that the Rebellion model – where a small number of people, typically from I.T. and Marketing conspire together to drag a retailer online – is already dead. In actual practice, a version which I'll call Sponsored Revolution seems to be alive and well. In its typical manifestation, there is indeed a general top-management mandate for adding new channels, but this does not translate into altering individual targets and KPIs, and so the implementation project team has to spend a disproportionate percentage of its effort wheedling co-operation out of the rest of the organisation. (See channel conflict in **Chapter 12**). To give a specific example, it is very difficult to persuade an individual buyer to devote 20% of his/her time to developing the range for online, or (worse) helping with product data management, when it is expected that only 3% of sales, and therefore 3% of his/her existing targets, will be met from online sales in the next 12 months.

The model recommended in the previous chapter falls into the Distributed class, and is where I would recommend that organisations should start out. A small dedicated team looks after driving the new channel(s), but has a clearly defined mandate to use certain resources from existing business teams. To use the same example, the buyer would have a specific target for new channel sales, and a clearly stated guideline regarding the expected time commitment.

Whether you implement something like the Focussed model depends on your appetite for matrix-managed style organisation design. In this model the channel team is dispersed back out into its wider departments again, but the idea of managing specific (usually just new) channels persists, usually with a skeleton coordinating team. For example, the team responsible for online customer-service would now report into general customer-services, but would still retain a distinct identity and a strong affiliation with the online channels.

Finally, we reach the point where the distinction between channels ceases, a true Multichannel organisation. For example there are not two groups of customers, there is one group of customers – "our customers" – and so the existence of a separate marketing team makes no sense. Yes there may be channel-centric technical specialists, for example experts in SEM or Affiliate Marketing, but every discipline has its technical specialists, and the task of management is to coordinate them towards achieving the same organisational goals.

In practice, retailers make these transitions at different speeds in different areas of the business. It's not uncommon to see something like Multichannel buying, Focussed marketing, and Distributed logistics. It's important that this is a deliberate choice, not an organisational accident or worse still a kind of Darwinian struggle for channel supremacy.

23.3   Practical Challenges

23.3.1 Broader roles

Similar to the introduction of any other new business process, various roles need to broaden, and this brings the challenge of whether to take a horizontal or vertical approach. To take a simple example, endless aisles imply extended ranges, usually with somewhat different characteristics from a typical store range (*Figure 75*).

Figure 75 - contrasting range profiles

In a well-designed multichannel proposition these two ranges will be complementary. Do you therefore make it one person's job to design the whole extended range, and perhaps therefore reduce the number of categories for which that person takes responsibility in order to re-balance the workload, or do you make it two separate tasks, risking losses of synergy (*Figure 76*)?

Option A – I liked 1992	Option B – 2 teams	Option C – 1 team
× lost sales	✓ simple organisation	× complex jobs
× lost customers	× planning in silos	✓ cross-channel plan
× long-term decline	× competing channels	✓ channel synergy

Figure 76 - organisational synergy or organisational simplicity?

Doing nothing (Option A) is not an option. Option C is plainly the most "multichannel", but it is also the most complicated. The core competence, in this case range architecture design, has not changed. You could argue that it is still only one range to be designed but with an extra dimension to the task, but even then the task has still become larger. One option which I have seen successfully used during the transition through the Focussed model is to keep the role as one, but to add an "advocate" for the extended range into the team, who is subordinate but accountable specifically for the success of the extended components. Such an advocate might span multiple ranges have multiples bosses; it's very "matrix management", and therefore not to the taste of those who prefer hierarchically defined accountabilities and management chains of command.

23.3.2 Clicks in traditionally bricks jobs

Back to the exasperating challenge of product data management again. Take a closer look at it. What does it involve? Well, it's very business process driven, standards and compliance are essential, flow management is important, just in time delivery is a core competence, it's about getting something from suppliers, and you are always working to serve demanding sales channels... sounds very like logistics / supply chain doesn't it?

Figure 77 - multichannel functions?

At first sight, product data management appears to be an additional competence, which arguably requires a completely new organisational unit to manage. There are lots of apparently new competencies which will be added to a typical retailer's team. SEM is obviously marketing discipline for example, but it isn't a traditional marketing skill. While keeping it separate might make sense in the early days, its budget very quickly needs to become part of the overall marketing budget – why should SEM have a ring-fenced budget? *Figure 77* extends this idea into product data management. Although the technical skills are quite different, the management competences are actually remarkably similar. ("Dear logistics manager, thank you for your letter of complaint regarding my suggestion that your team should…").

Whether you agree with this particular proposal or not (and I know of organisations who do indeed do this), the challenges of merging clicks skills like SEM into bricks teams like general marketing are another essential part of becoming truly multichannel in your organisation. Managing areas in which you do not yourself have experience and skills is one of the more difficult tasks for any manager. Seamlessly merging the old with the new to create a multichannel department, and ensuring that apparently competing demands of the new versus the old for budget, priority and resources are handled consistently with traditional old versus old debates, is a major but essential challenge.

23.3.3 New key performance indicators and targets

Channel conflict has already been the subject of its own chapter (*Chapter 12*). As the organisation moves through the phases of multichannel maturity, the ways in which this is resolved will need to keep changing (*Figure 78*).

Organisation Phase	KPI structures
Rebellion	In conflict! The quickest way to control (and then sponsor) the Rebellion is by implementing targets along the lines described in the Distributed model in the next line. At the very least, incentivise co-operation with this new thing, even if a full set of duplicated "for the other channel too" targets is not put in place.
Distributed	There will typically be "parallel" departments in some areas – online marketing and offline marketing for example. Each should have its own targets for its main channel focus, but each should also be given targets specifically around supporting the other channel(s). For example an offline campaign will *also* be measured around online success, and an online campaign not just measured on additional visitors to the website but also on additional visitors to stores (or some indirect but equivalent method, such as the increase in take-up of the online store-locator – incidentally this example is quite a common one).
Focussed	One department, with (equally important) targets for each channel. Specific individuals or sub-sections, whose job might be heavily weighted or exclusively focussed towards a particular channel, should have targets structured similarly to the Distributed model, but the overall function and its senior management should not.
Multichannel	One department, one target. When you have reached the point where it doesn't matter which channel a sale (or any other activity for

	that matter) is made on, then you have come full circle, and are measuring yourself in a fully multichannel way. In the "ideal" model, all individuals are also similarly multichannel in their roles and targets. Inevitably in practice, of course, more junior jobs will always have some particular focus which may be channel specific, especially more technical roles. Such jobs should continue to have parallel targets as in the Distributed model.

Figure 78 - KPI structure by organisation development phase

23.3.4 New budget relationships?

Obviously it's not realistic to give people new targets without giving them the resources to deliver to them. While this might just be indirectly budgeted resources like headcount, it might also involve cross-overs in direct budget accountability. In section **18.2** 'logistics is the new marketing', we considered a currently very visible situation; would you actually take this a step further and allocate some of that marketing budget to the logistics department, along with a sales-increment target to match?

Another real (i.e. some retailers have actually implemented it), but also illustrative example: a reasonably common accountability, and budgetary, switch along similar lines is in targets for returns rates in categories such as consumer electronics. A surprisingly high percentage of returns can be prevented by better information online (even if you don't have fully fledged eCommerce), access to better information in the call-centre, better information available to staff in-store – not just general information on policies, but specific information regarding product specifications, links to the online user guides typically available these days from most manufacturers, frequently-asked-questions. Maybe then the department accountable for product data management should also have the target, and associated budget, for waste? In some ways it is a very multichannel piece of organisational design: a function which at first sight looks like a new online function, actually responsible for a very old offline issue, and therefore targeted on building relationships with some of the most offline of all stakeholders – the traditional brick-and-mortar store management.

These examples also illustrate a secondary effect of multichannel: an increase in the number of *internal* organisational relationships that each stakeholder has. A potential benefit in accelerating towards a more genuinely multichannel organisation design is actually that the number of these relationships decreases again as a more conventional retail organisation model reasserts itself once more; in other words, although the roles get more complex, the actual organisation gets simpler (and possibly therefore slimmer and cheaper!) again.

23.3.5 New speed limit ahead

Figure 79 - multichannel culture clash?

Recently I helped a client select a new supplier to implement part of its new Multichannel I.T. platform. A noticeable feature of every single supplier presentation was a promise to use "hybrid agile methodology". Hybrid methodologies such as this example from I.T. are not caused by multichannel retail of course, but they are an interesting symptom.

A good reason for a retailer to consider holding their organisation at the Distributed stage is the culture clash, typically manifesting itself in differing expectations over the speed of change, between new (fast) and old (stable) channels. Partly this is a consequence of the differences in customer feedback cycle; tools such as online analytics mean that you can often see if a change to a website is working within 48 hours, and if it isn't you can reverse it. It's pretty difficult to do this with a brick-and-mortar store refit. The fact that it is so easy to use a suck-it-and-see approach in online channels means that planning is relatively a bit less important, and flexibility and responsiveness a bit more important, than offline.

The crunch comes when you start to implement genuinely multichannel propositions, such as click-and-collect, or endless aisle products which can be paid for at the same counter as in-store goods, and which therefore require change to be fully synchronised between offline and online. While such concepts can become a catalyst for organisational change, they are more likely to succeed if the change has been made first.

23.3.6 Devolution

We've covered Rebellion and Revolution, so how about a gentler option?

We highlighted earlier some important trends changing the service expectation of customers in stores. Two stand out in particular: firstly customers arriving much better informed, after having spent significant extra time on research than compared to what they would have done in the pre-multichannel world[102], which in turns leads to a need for better informed staff engaging in more sophisticated sales dialogues; secondly the freeing up of sales staff from static sales positions enabled by the use of wifi and tablet technology.[103] Both of these changes imply a step-change in the role of sales staff in store: from McJobs to iJobs, from mechanical cashiers to high-tech sales-people. Typically such changes are accompanied by a shift in emphasis from process to service, in terms of greater say in how things are done around here. This in turn potentially might lead by implication in flatter, more devolved, hierarchies.

---

[102] See for example, http://internetretailing.net/2012/12/multichannel-doubles-the-time-taken-to-make-a-purchase-study

[103] While everybody knows about Apple, retailers like JC Penney, hardly a high-tech bastion, have made a series of high profile announcements of plans in this area: see for example http://business.time.com/2012/07/20/a-store-without-a-checkout-counter-jcpenney-presses-on-with-retail-revolution/

It also leads in another critical multichannel direction: the need, and opportunity, to improve the customer experience by increased personalisation... which is the subject of the next chapter.

23.4   Top Takeaways

Customers must perceive one brand, one experience. A proactive organisation plan is required to ensure that a customer experience always appears multichannel.

A four-phase model describes retailers' evolution towards multichannel organisation: Rebellion (or Sponsored Revolution), Distributed, Focussed, Multichannel.

Rebellion: an organisational manifestation of channel conflict (*Chapter 12*).

Distributed: separate teams but with co-operating targets;

Focussed: joint teams but with channel-based targets;

Multichannel: one team, one target.

Practical challenges that may need to be overcome include: broader roles, clicks in traditionally bricks jobs, new KPIs, new budget relationships, blending different speeds of change and approaches to planning, more powerful roles at the customer-interface.

Chapter 24.   Personalisation

24.1   Introduction

Personalisation is not a new idea. Arguably it's been around since the invention of money and the establishment of the first shops; knowing your customers, offering them what they are most likely to want, and treating each as individually special to you have always been essential elements in the recipe for retail success. Remembering Mrs Ancient Greek's preference for black olives over green ones was just as important for Old Athenian Olive Stores as knowing my reading preferences is for Amazon today. Industrialising this from corner-store to multiple-outlet is not a new idea either. As soon as the data-processing power became available twenty to thirty years ago, many industries, especially financial services, realised that the information they already kept about their customers could be used to tailor their offers to the needs of each customer. CRM has a lengthy history, and in many ways personalisation is just the retail application of it.

The first industrial-scale personalisation schemes in retail were loyalty cards, whose objectives are usually loyalty second, data-capture first. Big Data is a popular buzzword in retail right now, but once again it's an idea with a past. The big loyalty schemes run by (for example) supermarkets have been generating huge quantities of data for years. This data has been exploited for both general insight into customer behaviour at a statistical level and for more specific personalisation of coupons and offers.

For the multichannel retailer, personalisation is critical because it makes it possible to follow the customer across all those steps in the purchase journey – from research to purchase, from smart-phone to store. At every step, the customer leaves a trail of history, and this trail can be exploited. The idea of personalisation is not complex. The challenge is to translate these broad ideas about "knowing our customer and treating them as individuals" and turn them into concrete actions and implementation plans. There are various standard families of techniques.

24.2 Techniques of Personalisation

24.2.1 DIY Personalisation

Take a look at the home-page of your smart-phone or PC or tablet. There's a familiar collection of icons and widgets on it. Now take a look at home-page of the person sitting just along from you. It's most probably an alien landscape: why's she not got the standard email application, how can she possibly have all that space taken up with that rubbish, what *has* she done to that menu option, how can anyone use a device with a background set to that colour? Despite its popularity – there are a lot of PCs and smart-phones, all customised by their users – this is not an idea that has found favour with retailers. Slogans such as shop your way[104] really mean shop *our* way, preferably drilling down to the products and offers we're particularly interested in promoting to you. Even Amazon doesn't let you mess with the layout of the store.

There are several reasons why this approach to personalisation isn't used much in retail. Customers in general don't use most individual retailers' digital channels often enough to make it worthwhile customising the store. Retailers spend a huge amount of effort optimising the user-experience of their channels, and giving the customer the opportunity to mess this up is likely to produce sub-optimal results. Most importantly, it is surprisingly difficult to implement from a technical perspective online (I can't think of any standard software solution that offers this option), and impossible in a brick-and-mortar environment unless you are in the "personal shopper" category of luxury retailing.

In summary, it's probably expensive project which will only succeed in reducing sales.

24.2.2 Simple Segmentation

The Old Athenian Olives Store in the introduction to this chapter was able to deduce its customers' preferences for colour of olives.

---

[104] Used for example by Sears in the US or Marks and Spencers in the UK

Being able to deduce anything about a customer relies on being to identify that specific customer and also remember and subsequently analyse his/her actions. The olive shop proprietor would do so by knowing his/her customers personally, watching their shopping over a few visits, and drawing a simple conclusion about customer segmentation – black only, green only, or both black and green olives.

In modern, multiple-outlet brick-and-mortar retailing, it isn't possible to know every customer personally. The typical solution is a loyalty card. A loyalty card involves a trade – the customer gets some sort of reward, in exchange for which the retailer gets to collect data about them. The retailer can analyse this data by itself, and in many countries can also purchase supplementary information (usually at street or postcode level, rather than individual customer level, for data protection reasons, but this granularity is generally sufficient). From this data, the retailer can make deductions about the customer – rich/poor, old/young, black/green-olive-eating – and place them in a segment. The segment can then be marketed to. For example by a coupon can be issued for a new juicier, flavoursome variety of green olive targeted at the richer, green-olive-preferring segment.

If you interact with your customers two or three times a year via brick-and-mortar channels only, this is probably about as good as it gets. You have to deduce the customer segments and then pro-actively market to them; too many segments are impossible to manage, and the effectiveness of the marketing becomes impossible to measure. This kind of simple pro-active segmentation can be surprisingly effective, but the key word is *simple*.

To go beyond simple, you need more data.

24.2.3 Complex Proactive Segmentation?

Creating a loyalty scheme which is worthwhile enough for a two-visits-per-year brick-and-mortar customer to join is something of a challenge (if you only spend twice a year, how long will it take to save up for a meaningful reward?), hence the existence of multi-branded loyalty schemes. The value for the customer multiplies as the participation of retailers (and other sectors of course) increases, and the deductive value of the data may increase for the retailer, although possibly its value may be limited by terms and conditions or local data protection laws.

Other retailers are fortunate enough to have much higher customer frequency. An average family might purchase several *thousand* items a year at a supermarket and visit weekly. Clearly a lot of segmentation is theoretically feasible, but how practical or commercially useful is it? And what relevance does all this have to Multichannel? Here's a lengthy recent quote from the CEO of Tesco, which encapsulates several important points:

"correlating the data we have with [other] sources of data – social networking data, mobile phone data, payment methods... and use that understanding to deliver an <u>even more personalised</u> offer... We're now making changes to our UK website to highlight promotions that are relevant to the customer who is browsing the site. Using Clubcard [loyalty card] data, we would show, for example, offers of our Everyday Value range to price sensitive customers, and offers of our Finest range to more upmarket customers. The power of this approach was born out by a test we did to sell mattresses. When a customer visited our website, we would use Clubcard data to tell us if the customer was more swayed by price or quality. We'd then display the type of mattress that best reflected that shopper's characteristic. <u>Sales grew by 10%</u>."[105] *[my underlinings].*

Firstly, the data sources are multichannel themselves – not just purchase history but social networking, mobile, and probably many others. In other words, even Tesco, with one of the most sophisticated purchase-history based analytical databases in the world ("you are what you eat" as they put it, which is itself a pretty succinct personalisation statement), feels the need to supplement this information. And a rich source of additional data is customers' online behaviour. Just consider the numbers briefly. A typical retail website

---

[105] Tesco CEO Philip Clarke, Global Summit of the Consumer Goods Forum, Istanbul June 2012

might have a conversion rate of 3% to 3.5% - say 30 visits per purchase – and a typical mobile site will be even higher, up to 100 visits per purchase. A customer in the research phase of his/her purchase might consider dozens of candidate products, each generating several page-views. Actually making a purchase and steering it through checkout requires further page-views (and explains the success of 1-click checkout). I have data from various retailers which suggests an average of around 200 page-views per cart, although of course it varies a lot by category. A customer making just two or three purchases online per year will leave a trail of several hundred data points.

Secondly, even armed with all this data, the proactive segmentation described basically just splits customers into cheap or posh. Doubtless Tesco's actual strategy was rather more sophisticated than a brief speech by the CEO at an executive conference can truly describe, but nonetheless this does illustrate an unavoidable limitation of this proactive segmentation approach: you can only realistically work with a handful of segments. The numbers quickly get out of hand. Cheap or posh, old or young, kids or childless, pets or none, drinker or teetotal, indigenous or immigrant... that's already 64 segments. Now invite your marketing or merchandising teams to come up with 64 different offers each time you want to do a campaign!

Thirdly, it works: a 10% uplift in sales should delight any retailer.

Fourthly, multichannel correlation of the kind suggested in the quote is only possible <u>if you can identify the customer consistently across all these channels.</u> Tesco here claims it is taking brick-and-mortar data, augmenting it with social networking data and mobile data, and then deploying this usefully to its website channel (**Figure 80**).

Figure 80 - Example Personalisation Data Flow

Tesco can do this effectively because it can use its loyalty card as an identity stamp on every channel the customer is interacting on, and has made it sufficiently worthwhile to the customer to take the trouble identify themselves (login/register online, present card offline). For many retailers it is difficult to offer sufficient advantages to the customer to identify themselves across channels in this way, and then technically very challenging to combine the data even it is available. A "single customer view" is an attractive concept on consultants' slides, but a very difficult implementation journey.

Lastly, being a supermarket with a loyalty scheme, Tesco already has a huge amount of essentially offline data available. For most retailers, the bias of data is the other way around – they can potentially capture a large amount of online data from website or smartphone, which they need to deploy at the right moments to influence the customer.

A 10% sales uplift is a big advantage. However the difficulties and disadvantages of this complex proactive technique – data bias towards online and/or limited data sets, reliance on customer identification, limitations in segmentation, huge databases – lead many retailers towards techniques which are single online channel specific and which are, in an apparent oxymoron, effectively anonymous personalisation.

24.2.4 Product associative personalisation

It is every retailer's dream to predict what their customers most want to buy, and offer it to them directly. Quite how difficult this is to do is exemplified by the famous Netflix prize[106], in which the online movie rental company offered a million dollar reward to anyone able to improve by 10% its existing algorithm to predict which movies a given customer would rate most highly. A read of the (mathematically) interesting papers describing the winning solution reveals the critical obstacle to such predictions – very small datasets about most customers' viewing/rating histories available to predict their satisfaction with a very wide range of possible movies.

The simplest strategy to overcome this is obviously to have bigger datasets. The problem for most retailers is that putting this simple step into practice requires a lot of purchasing history of reasonably characterising products, already stamped with some sort of customer-ID. Even if this data is available, then in practice this technique only really works very well in some categories such as media (books, movies, music downloads etc) and possibly fashion. In its simple form, it is just another variation on the simple customers who bought X also bought Y, just with a bit more complexity – customers who bought X and Y and Z over the last few months might like A or B. Importantly, this approach requires knowing nothing else about the customer except their purchasing history (which of course the customer has inevitably disclosed) – it is anonymous.

It's noticeable that Amazon themselves appear to have de-prioritised this kind of product associative personalisation which was once one of their flagship marketing tools. Instead they now tend to adopt a more route one approach. If you are ever unwary enough to browse a category without purchasing, for example, you will swiftly receive numerous prompts for products from that category, both via

---

[106] See www.netflixprize.com

mailings and "next time" you access their site. Yes, these are still cleverly personalised, but the basis is your expressed interest in the first place.

24.2.5 Real time personalisation

If "next time" seems a bit sluggish, how about "during"? It's important here to distinguish between engines which are genuinely profiling customers based on a history of activity over multiple visits, and those which are merely segmenting visitors based on information disclosed during a single session. That isn't to say both techniques may not be effective, but the latter applied to retail tends to drift back towards the rather easier (and cheaper) "customers who looked at X subsequently liked Y" techniques.

Dynamic visitor segmentation, based on information gathered during a single visit only, works especially well in sectors like travel. Deductions are made – for example have you expressed a preference for family holidays or not, long-haul or not etc – and the customer placed into some sort of segmentation tree (***Figure 81***).

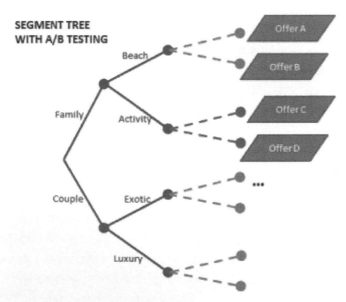

Figure 81 - Segmentation Tree Personalisation + A/B Testing

The segments are pre-defined during configuration, as are the possible offers. As with all A/B testing approaches, offer A or offer B is served at random to visitors who are classified as falling into that visitor-segment, and the site is dynamically tuned to favour serving the one which generates most favourable responses (the real-time nature may constrain this to simpler definitions of the response, such as just click-through, rather than the more complex goals typical of analytics such as actual checkouts).

24.2.6 Extended dataset personalisation

Personalising based on one visit to your website, or even on multiple interactions over several channels, might still leave you with an inadequate dataset about each customer to make meaningful deductions about them. Why not, then, use their interactions with other retailers – or in fact other interactions in general – to supplement this data? The best known users of this data-aggregation approach are the online advertising networks – a successful business model depends on displaying to users the adverts most likely to generate revenue for the ad-network i.e. the ones the user is most likely to click. The same logic works just as well for retailers – you use the same technique to predict what your customer is most likely to add to his shopping cart.

Strictly speaking it isn't the customer who is profiled by such data aggregation, it is the device (PC, smart-phone, tablet etc). In practice since the majority of customers don't share their device widely outside their close family, the effect is much the same. In fact, the reputable solutions in this space go to great lengths to avoid collecting information which could be considered genuinely personal - such as name or address – or jeopardise security – such as payment card details. Of course this is to avoid legal issues with data protection, but it is also because they simply don't need it; the technique is powerful enough at device level without trying to link the device back to its human user.

(Many of these data aggregation solutions rely on browser cookies, and the use of cookies is the subject of legislation in many countries, for example the EU cookie directive requiring sites to inform their users of the existence of such cookies and offer an opt-out. In practice only around 3% of users opt out, so the practical impact of legislation on the effectiveness of these techniques is extremely limited).

24.3   Issues

24.3.1 Into brick-and-mortar

The above account highlights the biggest issue with these techniques for the multichannel retailer – personalisation which is effectively anonymous or based on the device rather than the individual is all very well online, but rather less so when a human customer walks into one of your stores. There are two sides to this issue. On the one hand, many of the online techniques use sophisticated mathematical analysis to deduce facts about the customer which are totally self-evident face-to-face; most of us can tell whether someone is young or old without advanced technology to help us. There's nothing to then stop you propagating knowledge gleaned online – this type of customer prefers that model of product – into the brick-and-mortar environment, via training and promotional material.

On the other hand, a customer coming into a store after leaving a trail of online footprints is probably getting close to making a purchase decision. The rise of the ROBO-customer (research online buy offline) is one of the phenomena of the Multichannel age. Ideally you want your sales assistants ready-briefed to focus their efforts into dialogue and demonstration of products your personalisation algorithms have already predicted this customer is most interested in. Asking the customer to login to an in-store device to identify themselves, and then suddenly demonstrating a detailed knowledge of their browsing history might possibly be great customer service, but equally likely it might be perceived as creepy big-brother-like snooping. It might work on an in-store self-service kiosk, but in general self-service kiosks in store have a very poor track-record. It might possibly be an option on a sales-assistants' tablet device with very careful staff training. But the one time you can reliably ask the customer to identify themself is during checkout, and probably the most likely incentive for them to do so is the tried-and-trusty loyalty scheme. It's a case of better late than never, but it might create the opportunity to cross-sell at a time when the customer is at least in buying mode. (You also need an operating model in your stores that will allow an assistant completing a checkout to be free to also accompany a customer somewhere else to consider an additional purchase.) All roads tend to lead to Rome, in this case back to a loyalty scheme. Note that this does not necessarily mean a loyalty *card* – especially in the age of the smart-phone.

Alternatively you can take the broader multichannel view. A customer in store will most likely have researched any significant purchase online first: four fifths of Americans did so in 2011[107].This means that any personalisation solution in your online channels should have two sets of goals: firstly (of course) driving online checkouts; secondly, and possibly more importantly if you still have 90%+ of your sales taking place over the counter, a personalisation solution should be leading customers towards the product, or product options, they are most likely to finally evaluate and purchase when they arrive in-store. The latter is difficult, but definitely not impossible, to measure and should be an element of the business-case for any multichannel retailer considering personalisation strategy and solutions.

24.3.2 Not your data

So you've collected petabytes of data, analysed every customer in depth, personalised your online and offline experiences, and surmounted some minor legislative issues. What happens next? The answer in several countries is major legislative issues. Two quotes from the British government's Midata initiative:

"[Midata is] aimed at giving consumers access to the data created through their … internet transactions and high street loyalty cards."[108]

---

[107] Pewinternet.org
[108] UK government, department of business innovation & skills

"Midata will allow consumers greater insight into their everyday consumption and lifestyle habits by using applications and intermediaries to analyse their actual behaviours and thereby <u>empower them to make better spending choices and secure the best deals.</u>"[109] *[my underlining].*

One view of this the idea is that you surrender all that personalisation data back to the customer, and the customer then uses it to beat you up, especially on price. A more interesting longer term take is the notion that the customer will create their own personal profile of aggregated data, and make it available to you - the retailer – to allow you to customise the deal you want to offer them (*Figure 82*).

Figure 82 - Personalisation of the Future?

Although it might appear merely speculative, when there is a government initiative behind it, many possible partners already signed up, and retailers already beginning to advertise positions such as "Product Manager (My Data)", then it's certainly a trend to consider carefully when planning a personalisation strategy.

---

[109] www.bis.gov.uk

24.4   Implementation

Is a personalisation strategy worth all the effort? For the online pure-play retailer, the answer is almost certainly yes. Inevitably the data points are confusing, conflicting or self-serving, but a reasonable planning benchmark is that good online personalisation will increase sales overall by *at least* 15%. Actual gains might depend on how much you are already doing, since many sophisticated solutions also include simple features such top-sellers or basic recommendations that might come out of the box with your website.

Helpfully, and as usual with anything online, it is possible to measure the benefits directly. Furthermore, all the plausible suppliers of software or services provide straightforward A/B testing tools to compare your existing default approach with "their superior" results. Provided you are big enough to have some negotiating power, you might consider negotiating a price with them based on a cut of any proven sales uplift, at least for the first year or two after implementation. Not only does it remove a lot of the risk, but it also incentivises the supplier to do the best job possible; unlike many deals of this kind, it is simple online to measure the results objectively and to attribute only the directly achieved gains (thus preventing the supplier deriving unfair benefits from your other initiatives).

It is feasible to build simple segmentation solutions yourself, and in fact if you are new to personalisation, you might find it effective to begin this way. Quite a lot of the eighty-twenty rule benefits of personalisation can be gained from very simple segmentation of the cheap-or-posh kind. To go beyond this, it probably makes sense to purchase a service or solution. Delivering into multiple channels (including online channels such as email), personalising in real-time, complex algorithms, extended data sources, etc, are all challenges for which it is unlikely to make sense to reinvent the wheel.

For the multichannel retailer, any strategy needs to consider brick-and-mortar. As we have already seen, this might well imply a loyalty scheme of some sort in order to generate the data and identify the customer, which may not otherwise be a priority for your business.

The benefits of confining personalisation only to digital channels, via anonymous or device-based approaches, might well have sufficient positive benefit by itself, especially if online personalisation can also be proven to deliver sales uplift in stores.

24.5   Top Takeaways

Personalisation – changing the customer experience individually to draw each customer's attention to the things he/she is most likely to purchase – is not a new idea. When industrialising it, there is a family resemblance to CRM.

Reasonably reliable statistics suggest setting benchmark expectation of sales uplift at 10-15% at least.

Sales uplift should be directly measurable; when implementing a vendor solution, consider a shared-success deal.

Six technique families are identified here: DIY, simple segmentation, complex multichannel segmentation, product associative personalisation, real-time personalisation, extended dataset personalisation.

Personalisation techniques divide into two basic strategies: segmentation and anonymous personalisation.

Anonymous personalisation is more applicable to devices rather than individuals, and relies on devices not tending to be shared outside family groups.

Anonymous techniques depend on data volumes. Sources of data may include gathering data about the product set purchased or browsed, demographic or preference information supplied in real-time by the customer, and external sources information. The latter resemble the methods used by online advertising networks. In general, the more input data, the better the outcome.

Even simple segmentation with just two segments (e.g. cheap-versus-posh) may have significant benefits for small effort. Personalisation drawing on multichannel sources may only be appropriate for the biggest players with high participation loyalty schemes.

Letting the customer personalise his/her own experience (DIY) is not a technique that has found favour in retailing.

The biggest challenge for the multichannel retailer is always how to connect back to the human customer in the brick-and-mortar store. Loyalty schemes are one such option. Personalising only online channels via anonymous techniques may be the best option for those without a loyalty scheme.

Chapter 25. Mobile

25.1   Introduction

While a personalisation strategy might be optional, a mobile strategy is not. In any country where smartphone penetration has reached double digits, mobile is inescapable for retailers, even if you do not actually have, or even plan to have, an online sales channel.

In some countries, especially in the developing world, mobile is already the primary means to access the internet, measured by data volumes. Fixed line infrastructure is relatively sparse, and where it exists at all access is expensive relative to average incomes. Data from India in **Figure 83** suggests a tipping point midway through 2012 (although the data source is rather questionable and the graph should be treated as indicative only).

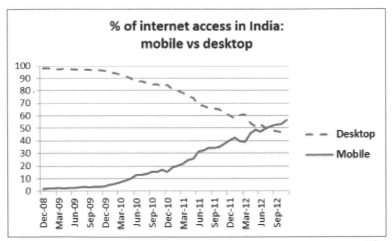

Figure 83 - internet access in India, mobile vs desktop[110]

Even in more developed countries with good quality fixed-line broadband available, access to the internet is rapidly mobilising (**Figure 84**); the outlier point in this data – China – reinforces the developing country story.

---

[110] Statcounter.com

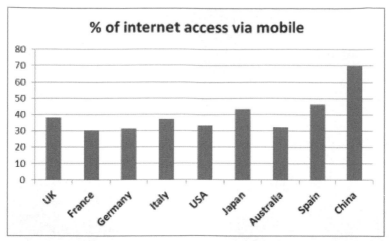

Figure 84 - % of internet access via mobile by country, October 2012[111]

The statistics in **Figure 85** (from the US) help to explain why these trends matter particularly for retailers. Mobile has become an essential part of the multichannel shopping journey (and its participation is growing all the time, so these figures will have increased by the time you are reading them).

Figure 85 - ROBO customers (research online, buy offline)[112]

However these same statistics also illustrate an essential consideration for a retailer planning a mobile strategy: "mobile" is a catchall term for several different types of device, principally smartphones and tablets, but more importantly small-screen or big-screen. Take a look at this schematic from an "old-fashioned" (i.e. non mobile) online retail screen - I took a screenshot from the category page of a retailer's website directly from my laptop and then overlaid it to capture the essential features of the page layout (**Figure 86**).

---

[111] Ofcom International Market Communications Report, December 2012
[112] Pewinternet.org, 2011

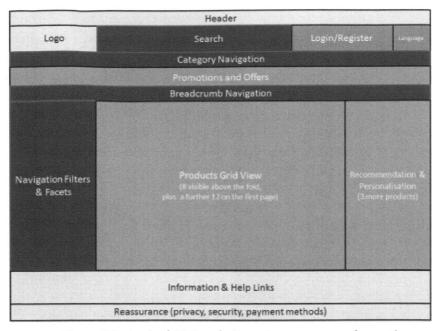

Header			
Logo	Search	Login/Register	Language

Category Navigation

Promotions and Offers

Breadcrumb Navigation

Navigation Filters & Facets	Products Grid View (8 visible above the fold, plus a further 12 on the first page)	Recommendation & Personalisation (3 more products)

Information & Help Links

Reassurance (privacy, security, payment methods)

Figure 86 - typical B2C website category page schematic

There are thirteen different basic sections, each of which contains multiple items of information. Eleven different products are fully or partially displayed before scrolling, including photographs and star-based ratings, plus further promotional items. I selected the retailer to use for this screenshot from amongst those whose online user-experience is generally considered to be best-practice. Translating this existing best-practice to a large-screen tablet is clearly not much of a leap; the same thing on a smartphone will be completely unusable. (This is also Google and Facebook's mobile dilemma – where do you put the ads?). So, where to start?

25.2   Requirements

25.2.1 Customer objectives: identifying relevant tasks in your customer journeys

As always with anything multichannel, the right place to begin planning is with your customers. Who are they, which ones have mobile devices, and what do they want to use them for? The same approach as already described in **Chapter 10** is still applicable for mobile: what are your preferred customer journeys, and what steps along the journey might *best* be served by mobile? That word "best" is very important: mobile purely for the sake of mobile is likely to cost more than it earns. Mobile for the sake of enhanced customer experience, however, drives sales, either directly or indirectly.

Once you have identified a set of potential customer uses, then next few subsections outline a basic decision tree to follow when laying out your mobile strategy.

25.2.2 Location

Mobile is exactly that: mobile. The opening question to consider is *where* the customer might be carrying out the potential tasks you have identified. Broadly these fall into five different spaces.

At home (or equivalents, such as in the office but using the device for non-work reasons): most probably the customer is using a mobile device for exactly the same tasks that they might use a PC, or especially a laptop, to perform. Your existing website, if you already have one, suitably optimised for mobile devices (see below) might well do the job.

At work for work-related reasons: many people have jobs on the move, and many of these jobs require on-the-spot research which might lead to a retail purchase decision. A niche example might be a plumber who needs to look up the right spare part to repair a broken boiler.

Generally on the move: sitting in a traffic queue or on a train is mobile time. Some directly retail purchasing activities, such as the weekly grocery shop, are ideal uses of this dead time. Otherwise, customers become just people: they want to be engaged and entertained.

In your stores: customers will be in mid-purchase research mode. Checking specifications, comparing products, and of course − unavoidably, so you may as well embrace it – comparing prices.

Near your stores: think mobile, think local. In fact the currently most popular use of a retailer mobile site or app is for its store-locator function. You probably put a lot of effort into driving traffic to your sites or stores – don't forget to plan to literally drive traffic!

A related, but rather critical question, is whether or not the task in question needs a real-time connection to the internet. If you are building up the weekly grocery shop, for later checkout, then no. If you are looking through a downloaded encyclopaedia of boiler-parts, then no again. But if you want to compare prices across multiple retailers, then definitely yes. If so, how fast does this connection need to be? Page-loading time matters just as much, if not more, on mobile as it does on conventional internet (see section *21.4* above).

25.2.3 Your objectives: marketing and/or transaction support?

What stage in the purchase funnel are you attempting to engage the customer? A mobile strategy can often logically split into two separate threads. The first thread will be aligned with your marketing strategy with separate elements associated with attraction, conversion and retention; the second more directly associated with transactions: information, price comparison, cart, checkout.

Mobile apps can be particularly effective at the attraction stage. Retailer mobile apps run the risk of being downloaded once, opened once, and then consigned to the lengthy list of scarcely used apps lurking on every mobile device. Engaging apps, that just happen to feature your brand and products, by contrast are likely to get a reasonable amount of re-use. Avoid the mistake of forgetting to give them some retail utility - showcasing your products, locating your stores, driving retention or reactivation - in favour of being purely entertaining.

Coupons and vouchers are an excellent use of mobile to enhance conversion. Unlike their paper equivalents, mobile coupons don't get lost, are difficult to forge, and with the right technology can be validated at the point-of-sale in store. They can be issued dynamically in real-time based on trigger events such as customer near the store, excessively quiet Tuesday afternoon for general footfall, competitor event. Their redemption can be tracked afterwards for subsequent measurement and retention remarketing.

General mobile payment as a conversion-enhancing option appears tempting at first sight, but in many countries right now the best advice is probably to wait a while (but not all countries – mobile payment is essential in Japan for example, and some developing countries such as Kenya have SMS-based schemes with surprisingly high take-up). The landscape of payment schemes and standards in most countries could best be described as confusing, which drives a vicious cycle where consequently consumer take-up remains rather low, and so it would be very easy for a retailer to make a significant investment betting on the wrong horse. (Apple's schizophrenic attitude to its Passbook application whilst omitting a near field communication chip from the iPhone5 is a good illustration of the current state of play). If I come to rewrite this paragraph at the start of 2015, I fully expect to have to replace it with a whole section.

Transaction-enhancing mobile as a whole requires overcoming an additional challenge: the complexity of the user experience that can reasonably be delivered on the device.

25.2.4 Complexity

Take another look at *Figure 86*. That web-page is a surprisingly complex thing, and that's just one sub-stage in an overall purchase journey. There might also be home-pages, product pages, information pages and most complex of all, cart and checkout pages. On each page, the user has a choice of many ways to proceed. If your target task, location and purpose expect that the customer will be using their smartphone, then such complexity is simply impractical. Interaction with a smartphone needs to take place in bite-sized chunks, with only a few diversionary options available, on simple screen layouts. A moderately greater level of complexity is possible via an app than via a smart-phone web-browser, but realistically the complexity-bar remains low even on an app.

There are further implications to this. Your existing online presence will require modification for smartphone users. Your website is still accessible via a smartphone web-browser, and you cannot afford it to appear unusable. You will have invested significant time and effort in making an existing website optimal for your customers, and you don't want to throw that away just because many of them are now using their smartphone instead of their PC or laptop. Inevitably, this leads to a need for responsive or adaptive design (see below); the site needs to detect the type of device being used to browse it, and change its presentation accordingly.

You may also decide that some interactions which are appropriate via a PC browser don't belong on a smartphone. This is particularly true of checkout and especially the payment sub-step. A classic customer journey change is when click-and-collect (see **Chapter 26**), implemented with pre-payment during the checkout on a PC browser, is changed to reserve-and-collect with payment in-store when translated to a smartphone. There are two benefits to this change: the checkout journey is simplified to help it through the smartphone; it overcomes the continuing reluctance of customers to provide payment details to mobile devices[113]. There is, however, a corollary – associated business processes have to be changed. Continuing the click-and-collect example, a payment step may now be required during the collection process.

25.2.5 Omni-channel

Reserve-and-collect is one situation where mobile plays a part in a longer, truly omni-channel multistep connected customer journey. Another common example is the omni-channel shopping cart/basket. Mobile is a great channel for research, but a difficult channel for final

---

[113] See for example http://www.paymentssource.com/news/Mobile-Payments-On-Rise-But-Many-Consumers-Wary-About-Security-3009979-1.html although be warned that published statistics in this area are particularly variable, changing continuously and often more-than-usually country-specific

checkout. A brick-and-mortar checkout like reserve-and-collect is one option. What about online?

Connecting online channels typically requires two things. The first is a common login. Implementing a shared login benefits the customer some, but benefits the retailer more: it helps solve a key challenges in implementation your personalisation strategy (see *Chapter 24*). The second is typically a shared-channel shopping cart. Customers don't just use shopping carts as a checkout vehicle; even on sites with helpful features like wish-list or save-for-later, customers often prefer to use the cart itself as a scratchpad to save items of interest for further research, and then eventual selection and checkout. Ensuring that the cart can be shared between mobile (research) and PC/laptop (selection and checkout) is an essential step to capturing customers on this particular journey.

25.3   Implementation

25.3.1 From requirements to implementation

The link from requirements to implementation strategy is summarised in *Figure 87.*

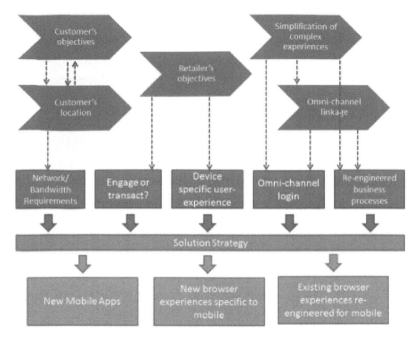

Figure 87 - Mobile strategy, schematic from requirements to solution

Having mapped out your candidate set of customer requirements, including changes to your existing proposition or business processes, you are then in a position to consider them from an implementation perspective.

25.3.2 Do you need apps?

An issue to be addressed early in planning mobile implementation is whether or not you propose to create any mobile apps, or whether a browser-based approach alone will be sufficient. I would suggest that your approach *as a retailer* is to take a default position that you will not create apps, and then seek to justify whether any exceptions are appropriate. An individual retailer should start from a position that it is not inherently compelling or useful enough to justify special place on its customers' mobile devices. The challenge to any proponent of a retailer-specific app should be to demonstrate that this is wrong.

What criteria might an app proponent employ in support of the need for an app? A starting list should include:

Necessary **complexity**. Complexity which is merely desirable is almost certainly complexity which is unnecessary and which you should be considering how to engineer out of your multichannel proposition in any case. Necessary complexity might arise if you have, for example, sophisticated configurable products with many options. Working through these within the confines of a smartphone screen will be challenging for your customers, and subjected to the limitations of browser capabilities will be doubly so. In fact an app may well be a better solution altogether than any browser, including those on a laptop or PC as well as mobile.

Compelling engagement. If your chosen objectives are less transactional and more focussed on engagement, and by implication entertainment, then an app is probably a better option. Nevertheless you should remember that the average lifetime of an app, from download to neglect, is brief; some reports suggest it is under 30 days[114]

Offline operation. Self-evidently, if your customer task is expected to be performed when an internet connection is unavailable, then an app is probably the only option. Continuing the example used above, when someone has his/her head – and phone – inside a boiler while validating the specification of possible replacement parts then a high-quality connection is unlikely to be available.

Complex memory. Logged-in browser sessions, and cookies, can of course remember things. But if your task requires a large amount of option setting and personal configuration, then an app is more likely to be the right option.

Developing an app is probably a more expensive option with less likelihood of customers using it; you need concrete reasons of the kind listed to justify the additional investment.

---

[114] See for example: http://techcrunch.com/2009/02/19/pinch-media-data-shows-the-average-shelf-life-of-an-iphone-app-is-less-than-30-days/

25.3.3 Multiple devices

One of the happier aspects of being a web-developer for several recent years has been the uniformity of the user-interface device that needs to be supported. When aiming only at PC/laptop browser sessions, it has generally been acceptable to target a maximum of two or three display sizes. Furthermore, although the idiosyncrasies of the different browsers – and their apparent inability to adhere consistently to standards, especially CSS and DOM model – can occasionally be exasperating, it is rarely more than a nuisance. Enter the mobile device. Now even a simple browser interface may have to cope with multiple screen densities and sizes, from cramped early smartphones to the latest tablets, which might then be operated in either portrait or landscape mode (or worse, in both modes), support widely variable features and capabilities, while still continuing to successfully support PCs, laptops and notebooks.

Assuming you have an existing website, adding support for mobile is likely to be an early priority. One way to do this is to build different sites for different devices, detecting the device-type when the user first arrives and redirecting. Sites whose name suddenly changes from 'www.xyz.com' to 'm.xyz.com' when accessed from a mobile are typical of this approach. The upside of this option is that it usually does not require significant technical changes or reskilling of IT teams, and implementation is reasonably quick-and-dirty. Two approaches are typical. The first is the obvious build two (or more) parallel sites. The second, which involves much less up-front labour but has significant downsides including potentially poor performance and compromised user-experience, is to use a supplier/tool which will (semi-)automatically re-render your site for mobile.

The more strategic solution is to implement *responsive design*. This rather elusive technical term basically means ensuring a single page caters for the layout – essentially shape and density – of all the devices that might access it by responding to the needs of each device. Longer term this offers many advantages, not least that a particular page (a product or promotion for example) retains a single url for external sites such as social media to link to. Shorter term, it's more disruptive than the duplicate site approach because your existing site has to be rebuilt at the same time, probably by IT teams/suppliers who also need to adapt to a different skillset.

The challenge in all this is that this might not merely mean a screen-by-screen reshaping; fundamental changes to the user journey could be required. If this is genuinely the case, it's possible that an app might once again be the better option. Not that building apps presents any less of these device-centric challenges. The basic size/density issues are still present. You then have to build for at least Android, Apple and probably Microsoft at minimum, which is not simply customising slightly for different browser versions, but means a complete rebuild from the ground up in three different technologies.

Finally there is *adaptive design*[115] to consider: what capabilities does the device have? For example do you want to use the inbuilt GPS, does your interface want to support pinch-gestures on the touch-screen? If so, what happens on devices without this particular capability? This is typically a rather bigger issue for apps than browser-based interfaces although it applies to both; users have lower expectations of a browser interface, and a minimum-standard is probably acceptable.

25.3.4 Tabula Rasa

Not the name of the next generation mobile tablet, but Latin for 'clean slate'. Mobile is overtaking PC/laptop as the preferred method of accessing the internet. In India and China it already has. In Western Europe or the US, the cross-over is expected in the next few years (the consensus average seems to be 2016). If you already have an existing web presence then you face the challenge of adapting it for mobile, with all the issues described in the previous sub-section.

---

[115] Both responsive design and adaptive design are generally understood terms, but which lack a formal accepted definition. Adaptive design, in particular, is a term whose meaning can vary more widely than the suggested description given here.

What if you don't? This situation is more likely the less developed the market you are in. And in less developed markets, internet access via mobile is likely to be more-and-more the preferred method. Even if you are operating in a developed market, if you don't already have a serious website, why would you build one aimed at what will soon be a minority of users, and play catch-up with your competitors? The obvious way forward is to reverse priorities: start from mobile – in particular smartphone – customers, and only second worry about those old-fashioned PC or laptop users.

25.4   Top takeaways

A mobile strategy is not optional. In developing markets, mobile devices are already the primary means of accessing the internet. In more developed countries, this cross-over is expected within the next two to three years.

Your existing website is already visible on mobile devices. If it doesn't look good on a small smartphone screen, you have a problem.

If you are planning multichannel in a less developed market, consider a mobile-first, desktop second strategy.

Five important factors to consider when planning mobile strategy requirements: customer objectives, location, engagement-versus-transaction, complexity, omni-channel link-up.

Consider what steps in the customer journey might *best* be served by mobile.

Where is your customer? At home, at work and using a mobile device for work reasons, on the move, in your stores, near your stores?

Engagement marketing might need a separate mobile strategy thread from transactional support.

Mobile payment may be a wait-and-see situation in most markets. Mobile coupons or vouchers, however, may already be an excellent tool. Solutions which validate them directly at the checkout and make their redemption available for analysis and re-marketing are already available.

Interactions on smartphone screens must necessarily be simpler than on large-display devices. This may necessitate amending some of the flow of the customer journey – for example deferring click-and-collect payment-step from click to collection.

Five important factors to consider when planning mobile strategy implementation: connectivity and bandwidth requirements, engagement level, device specific experience, omni-channel (especially login), re-engineered business processes.

Browser versus apps: a retailer's default should be browser. Apps might be justified by the need for: *necessary* complexity, compelling engagement, offline operation, complex memory.

Temporary re-engineering of an existing website may be achieved by duplicating/redirecting, or by tools which re-render. Longer term, responsive and adaptive design should be considered. <u>The definition of both terms is still evolving</u>.

Responsive design (suggested definition): ensuring each page caters for the layout of any device that might be accessing it, by changing itself to fit.

Adaptive design (suggested definition): adapting the user experience to fit the capabilities of the device. For example does it support GPS, or pinch-gestures?

Chapter 26.   Click-and-Collect

26.1   Why offer it?

Customers like click-and-collect (pick-up-in-store). Reliable public domain data points are more than usually elusive, but a hunt through public statements made over the last 12 months or so by top multichannel retailers in the UK shows the following picture (*Figure 88*).

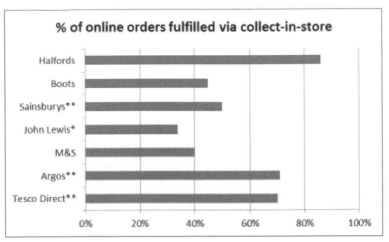

Figure 88 - online orders via collect in store statistics

Some notes: figures marked ** exclude "impossible" articles such as beds or large freezer cabinets and also exclude grocery; figures for John Lewis (*) are for orders placed on the John Lewis website but collected in sister brand Waitrose's stores, therefore actual John Lewis figures are much higher. Sainsburys also observes that the percentage of general merchandise orders collected in store rises from 50% to around 75% during the Christmas peak.

Customer reasons given for this popularity include mistrust of delivery services (which explains the Sainsbury seasonal peak), improved convenience due to being able to choose when to collect, and of course dislike of shipping charges; it is very difficult to justify a shipping charge for a collect-in-store order. However even retailers who offer free shipping see high rates of collect-in-store. Furthermore, take-up is usually very rapid. The 40% of Marks and Spencer's orders fulfilled in this way was a level arrived at after only around a year of offering the service.

Not only do customers appreciate click-and-collect, but retailers do too:

"We are seeing about <u>34% of those visits translating into additional sales in shop</u> and that number is growing exponentially at the moment. It's typically or increasingly for purchases that the customer didn't think they would make. So it is quite outwith [beyond] whatever they were going to collect."[116] [my underlining].

It isn't so often that you can find a service that customers actively like, that generates incremental sales from one customer in every three, and that offers a chance to differentiate from online pureplays all rolled into one!

26.2   Implementation

One extra stakeholder group that is fan of click-and-collect is consultants, because planning it can be used to illustrate many of the concepts and issues of multichannel retail. To begin with, it is a particularly clear example of proposition differentiation by convenience (**Chapter 8**), as well as something truly multichannel where brick-and-mortar combined seamlessly with online has a genuine advantage over either channel separately. In turn, planning its implementation brings together several of the essential concepts we have discussed in this book (**Figure 89**).

Figure 89 - click-and-collect planning flow

26.2.1 Available to Promise

See **Chapter 16**. The most fundamental question to consider when planning a click-and-collect proposition is where you will pick the order, and therefore what stock (and by implication service level) you

---

[116] John Lewis, September 2011

will promise to the customer. The immediate reaction – you've already shipped stock to your stores, surely you should pick it there – is not necessarily the right one. In fact the majority of click-and-collect implementations pick their orders in a central fulfilment centre exactly like home-delivery orders, and then ship them to the stores. There a several reasons for this, at first sight illogical, choice including the following.

Confidence in the promise: most retailers have minimal or non-existent back-of-store warehousing areas. The best place for in-store stock is where customers can see it and buy it, out on the shop floor. If an online order arrives in the store, can you be confident that the stock will be out there when you come to try and pick it? For many retailers, the answer is no: stock control accuracy or shrinkage might already be an issue; high velocity retailers can expect a percentage of stock to be in customers shopping carts and therefore neither available nor booked-out at point-of-sale; stock-control units might be in shipping units not individual items.

Picking process quality: a specialist fulfilment centre will devote a high proportion of its working time and business process investment into ensuring that orders are accurately picked. It is difficult to replicate this in store. Although in theory errors can be easily corrected in store, in practice many customers do not actually check the contents of their order item-by-item during the collection process.

Endless Aisle SKUs: if your multichannel proposition includes an endless aisle, then some or all of the products a customer might order will not be in store. If part of an order cannot be picked in the store, why not pick all of it anyway in the specialist fulfilment centre, where you are more likely to pick it right?

Reservation of stock: some retailers find it very difficult to physically separate out stock reserved for customer orders from stock generally on sale.

Paperwork: an online order, even one collected in store, requires some associated paperwork (see *Chapter 20*). Equipping stores to print this paperwork may be difficult.

If these issues can be overcome in your organisation however, then picking in store offers two important advantages. It's basically simpler, and it's definitely faster: you can make very aggressive customer promises – order online, ready to collect in an hour – which might be an advantage depending on your location and customers. Although it's not a retail example, takeaway pizza is a simple case-study where all the above issues are easily overcome and a timely promise makes a big difference.

26.2.2 Online checkout changes

If you are planning to pick from a central warehouse, then the changes required are fairly simple. There needs to be an option for the customer to locate and specify a collection store in addition to the existing dialogue to provide a delivery address. (If you are proposing to use a local collection partner service like Relais Colis in France, then these pick up points need to be included too. For most purposes, such services appear to the retailer almost the same as home delivery – they are not click-and-collect for the purpose of this chapter).

If you will also offer pick-up in store, then checkout becomes more complicated. Standard practice is to invite the customer to specify a location, and then display possible nearby pick-up destinations in a matrix of available-to-promise somewhat like *Figure 90*.

	Buda Store	**Pest Store**	
Product A	In Stock	In Stock	Click here to see other nearby stores
Product B	In Stock	In Stock	
Product C	X	In Stock	

Figure 90 - pick-up in store checkout availability matrix

The critical objective is to avoid the leading the customer into a never-ending journey of "no, not in stock there either, why don't you have another guess?" by at least displaying several plausible options on a single screen.

This is a relatively busy display, and so adapting it for smartphone display requires some care. Busy customers on the move – mobile customers – are the most likely to use a click-and-collect service, so this is definitely one screen that repays careful device-specific design (see **Chapter 25**). Having successfully persuaded the customer to navigate this, getting them through payment options may be a screen too far, which helps explain why pay-on-collection might be especially suitable for smartphone users.

26.2.3 Shipping

If your choice is to pick in a central fulfilment location and then ship to stores, the shipping method becomes an issue. Mixing customer parcels with bulk distribution challenges is a step too far for many retailers' logistics; typically only those whose range consists of items which ship in large individual boxes or those who operate a cage-distribution network can easily blend bulk and parcel shipping together. The rest will use a similar shipping method as for parcel home-delivery, although of course it makes sense to try and negotiate some processes and discounts when several parcels will be consistently moving each day to a well-defined set of store locations.

If you have chosen an aggressive promise – order today, collect tomorrow – then it may be necessary to be quite specific about timings. The order not only has to arrive in store, it has to be recognised, probably logged, and taken to a collection point. A closer look at many retailers promises reveals statements like "order by 6pm, collect after 2pm tomorrow", which gives enough time to pick centrally, ship to store during the morning, and register and file before a customer can come and collect.

26.2.4 Payment policy

If you already have a payment-on-delivery policy (see **Chapter 20**), then there's not too much to change. Amending this to pay-on-collection requires only minor changes to your order lifecycle.

Ensuring that your point-of-sale is able to take payments for parcels of goods whose price was determined yesterday on the website may require some modifications. Most retailers do not scan individual SKUs at collection. Not only do customers not necessarily want to open up parcels already nicely packed for collection and transport, but for many retailers scanning this "non-store" stock would create unacceptable complications in replenishment or financial systems. If you don't want to start with a fully integrated systems solution, then answer is typically to scan a pre-printed whole-order pricing barcode on the invoice or parcel.

Collect-in-store orders have a higher risk of customer no-shows. If you just incurred all the costs of shipping the parcel to the store, without being able to charge a shipping fee, and the customer then fails to turn up, this can be expensive and irritating, doubly so if the products are from the endless-aisle range and therefore not easy to put back on the shelves. Payment-on-despatch or payment-on-order might therefore be preferred to payment-on-collection; a customer perception that they have already paid discourages no-shows, even though ultimately a refund would be forthcoming in any case.

Payment-on-despatch mixed with not picking in store requires a tricky technical issue to be resolved: when actually did the despatch happen? I'll risk a recommendation here: the despatch happens when the goods leave the central fulfilment warehouse, consistently with the despatch of orders for home-delivery. Moreover from the perspective of your financial systems, the goods are no longer "stock", they are parcels which the customer already owns. You are just a shipping agent and your stores now have a secondary role as post-offices. Set up your financial systems and processes accordingly.

Having a different payment policy for collect-in-store orders compared to home-delivery orders is really only practical if you will ensure that customers cannot place split orders – some goods to be collected, some to be delivered, altogether in the same order. This is less an issue of available-to-promise, more an issue of checkout usability. The most likely situation where this might arise is if you prefer pay-on-collection for orders from a smartphone while sticking with pay-on-order or pay-on-despatch from other channels. You have to balance between potentially lost sales by restricting the customer in this manner versus the complexity which would arise from split orders with mixed payment policies: simplicity usually wins this argument every time (especially in your IT department).

26.2.5 Other order lifecycle issues

No-shows are the big downside of collect-in-store; they're like returns but with additional costs and complexity. Minimising their frequency is worth some investment. It makes sense to send frequent messages to the customer – this is one situation where the use of SMS is wholly legitimate – to remind them to collect.

The related question is how long to hold the items in store before treating the customer as a no-show. The minimum realistic minimum is seven days: the customer has chosen collection in order to choose a time convenient to them, and since most people's lives are built around weekly cycles, ensuring a complete week is available for collection makes sense. Good practice is probably therefore 14 days, allowing the customer to miss a week, assuming space constraints permit. In practice, the majority of customers will collect within 72 hours.

26.2.6 Fraud prevention

First the opportunity: a collecting customer needs to show some ID, solving lots of the multichannel identification challenges described in the chapter on personalisation (*Chapter 24*). In fact the collection process can be really omni-channel, with an online order from a PC being collected in a brick-and-mortar store supported by a mobile proof-of-order and a paper ID following a telephone reminder from the call-centre.

The corresponding problem is that proof of ID requirement. If your payment policy is pay-on-order or pay-on-despatch, then it is necessary to take steps to prevent fraud. All click-and-collect propositions require both proof of order (confirmation message printed out or on shown on mobile) plus proof of ID to be shown. If you want someone else to collect, then either that person has to show your ID as well as theirs, or you have to specify exactly who will collect at the time you place the order.

26.2.7 Collection desk

The first question is location. There is obviously a minimum space requirement, including secure storage for parcels. Assuming you have some choice, then location is a choice between maximising convenience for the customer – preferred parking and a desk location near the door – versus maximising incremental sales for the retailer – usually a location requiring the customer to walk through as much of your casual takeaway assortment as possible. Incremental sales usually win this battle.

Secondly, remember that customer behaviour at the point of collection can vary. Some customers will simply take their parcel and leave. Some will (hopefully) bring additional purchases made in store to check out. Some will open their parcel at the counter; if there are issues with it, you are faced with instantaneous customer service requirements for replacement, refund or advice. In retailers where collect-in-store traffic is not big enough to justify a separate desk, a natural merger is between any existing customer desk and the collection desk, partly because the additional customer service skills overlap so much.

26.3　Top Takeaways

Customers like click-and-collect. Take-up is usually rapid, and retailers who offer it typically see 30-50% of all online orders fulfilled via this route.

Click-and-collect generates genuine incremental sales in store. This book includes two specific quoted data points from retailers: 25% and 34% of customers who collected-in-store made an unplanned additional purchase.

Planning decisions in implementation include: available-to-promise (pick in store/pick centrally); online checkout changes; shipping;

payment policy; no-show policy; fraud-prevention and ID; collection desk location and processes.

Pick-from-store offers advantages in simplicity and customer promise. Its issues include confidence in the promise; picking process quality control; endless aisle (non-store) SKUs; stock reservation; paperwork printing.

Checkout dialogue needs be carefully modified to avoid infinite loops. A decision is needed regarding split shipping options (collecting only part of the order). Checkout can become complex.

Pay-on-delivery translates easily into pay-on-collection. However no-show rates will be higher, potentially exposing you to significant extra costs.

If you are offering the service on smartphone, you may choose to deliberately simplify the checkout, including switching mobile orders to a pay-on-collection policy.

A collection desk is required, which tends to be located at the back of the store. Customer handover processes, which may include ID validation and paying for additional purchases, overlap significantly with existing in-store customer service desk duties, and so many retailers double-up.

Chapter 27. Clearance

27.1 Background

A frequent problem facing retailers of any kind is in clearing old stock. There is an inevitably unpleasant write-down to handle, and probably an adverse impact on margin targets. The challenge, then, is to find an efficient channel to clear the stock, and minimise the margin hit and write-down impact. Many retailers implement clearance tabs on their websites via a separate parallel taxonomy branch. These can be linked to seasonal sale events and can be excellent drivers of traffic and cross-sales.

However an alternative, implemented by many retailers, is to use eBay, Amazon or other online marketplaces – to use another additional channel as part of their overall multichannel approach. This keeps the clearance stock out of stores/off the main website, reduces negative brand messages, and also potentially allows an efficient route to clear "second quality" stock. The catalogue retailer Argos, for example, is one of the biggest Sellers on eBay UK – driven in part by its constant need to clear supply chain space to make room for the next catalogue.

At first sight, however, marketplaces look like expensive channels. On eBay for example, by the time eBay listing fees and commissions, plus probably PayPal fees, have been charged, the total commission will average around 11%. Amazon Marketplaces, for typical sales volumes, is comparable or more expensive. Other marketplaces such as China's TaoBao - which includes its own PayPal equivalent in Alipay – or Poland's Allegro are no cheaper. Why would you want to use a channel taking a further 11% in fees against products where you are already taking painful margin hits, when you've already investing in implementing your own online sales channels?

27.2 Analysis

For products which are reasonably in demand, sold via an online marketplace which has a sufficiently large number of Buyers (i.e. any that you might reasonably choose), the marketplace will operate fairly close to optimal price-efficiency.[117] In plain English, on a busy marketplace things sell for what they are worth.

A concrete example will help (and I'm going to refer to eBay, rather than the generic term auction marketplace, in the interests of simplicity). Suppose you have an article originally priced at $100 but which you are now obliged to put into clearance. Evidently it wasn't "worth" $100 after all in the eyes of your customers. Feed a steady supply into eBay, without flooding the market, and you might reap an average selling price of say $70, with minor variations around this average. eBay will then take its various fees out of this, leaving you with an average net price of perhaps $62. Suppose instead of using eBay, you decide to use a clearance section on your own site. What price should you ask for the same product? The answer of course is somewhere between $62 and $70, a kind of goldilocks zone where the price is not too high, not too low. Price it above $70 and you'll be undercut by the marketplaces and your rate of sale will be low; customers prepared to buy clearance goods are probably also marketplace customers. Price it below $62, and you will make less money than you would have done via eBay (Figure 91 - Goldilocks price range for clearance).

Figure 91 - Goldilocks price range for clearance

---

[117] eBay, formally defined as a Second Price, English Auction, Fixed End-Time marketplace, is the subject of numerous (mathematically) interesting academic studies. See for example www2008.org/papers/pdf/p925-huA.pdf. A general summary of their conclusions is that marketplaces are not quite properly efficient in a purist sense, but for products in common circulation whose value is reasonably understood by enough bidders, then they are sufficiently price-efficient for the purposes of this book!

The problem is that you can only know this optimal goldilocks price after seeing the auction price for this product before placing on clearance. How easily can you predict it, and therefore do better via your own clearance? Well, firstly you might be able to do so by watching similar items auctioned on eBay. Of course eBay is not absolutely a perfect market, so you would have to watch a series of auctions and take a reasonable average. For most retailers, this is impossibly labour intensive.

Secondly, you might just price the item at more than $70 anyway. In fact, if you have a very small stock-holding of this item, and reasonable traffic to your clearance channel, this is a sensible policy. Not every customer is a "perfect" customer in the sense of optimising price, and in fact experience in non-price transparent retailing environments shows that the prices paid by a customer are (more-or-less) normally distributed. So if you only have a small stock-holding, and can wait long enough for a non-price sensitive customer, you can maximise your clearance this way. (Discussions of buy-it-now pricing on eBay generally recommend that this should be 15-25% higher than you expect to realise via auction).

Thirdly you might be skilled enough to price in the goldilocks zone – exactly between $62 and $70. This is unlikely at the first attempt, but if you have the systems and processes to monitor rates of sale and dynamically vary prices accordingly, then although you might make a few under-pricing mistakes early on, if you can react to these fast enough, then you are better setting your own price via your own clearance channel. Note that "fast enough", in an online environment with a bargain to be spotted and circulated quickly via social media, might be a matter of hours.

Otherwise, you are, in fact, better off paying eBay, or some other auction site, their commission in exchange for their highly liquid, "perfect" market, optimising your return on the sale. Alternatively, you could use non-auction retailer marketplaces like Amazon Marketplaces. Amazon operates, in effect, a reverse (or Dutch) auction. Sellers bid down, until a lowest consensus price is reached. In the clearance scenario envisaged, this is in fact quite bad for you as the Seller. The problem is that this Dutch auction takes place, with complete transparency, and without a committed purchaser at the end of it[118]. So the buyer can cherry pick. The optimal buying strategy is, in effect, to wait for a seller to make a mistake. As a seller, you are bound to do worse than you would via eBay, unless your commission advantage is significant on Amazon. In practice the difference may be more theoretical than practical, as eBay buyers may well base their buying valuations on Amazon marketplace published prices anyway.

However there is another factor to consider before finally selecting the best channel for your clearance: the secondary incremental costs of marketplace selling. Many apparently "additional" tasks, such as listing, can be automated, and others, such as photography and product description can re-use the assets you already created to sell these articles online in the first place. The same logistics processes can probably be reused with only minor modifications. However some differences generate truly incremental costs, most especially customer contacts. Marketplaces switch the bias of customer-contacts from post-sale to pre-sale. Moreover the customer-contacts-per-order ratio for a marketplace sale is typically between three and five times greater than the same ratio on a conventional B2C site, albeit mainly via the cheaper channel of email. Success on a marketplace is strongly correlated to reputation, which means you also need to respond promptly to all these additional contacts. Marketplaces are extremely unforgiving of sellers who attempt to economise on service.

27.3   Top Takeaways

Marketplaces offer an alternative clearance option, at a high cost in fees. Many retailers, however, find them an effective option despite the apparent cost.

Should your retailer use a marketplace for clearance?

Yes: if the quantity of stock of a particular SKU is relatively high;

---

[118] It is not fixed end-time

No: if you only want to clear a small quantity of stock, have an alternative sale channel, and can afford to wait for a less price sensitive customer to come along;

Yes: if you do not have the time to invest in finding the goldilocks price in advance;

Yes: if you cannot afford the systems or time to highly-dynamically price yourself;

No: if you cannot handle 3-5x the customer contacts-per-order you normally expect, albeit by email;

Yes: if your brand strategy finds a marketplace channel acceptable;

No: if the additional traffic generate from the clearance section on your existing online channels generates significant cross-sales.

Chapter 28.   Online Grocery

28.1   Background

At first glance, online grocery should be a huge opportunity. Grocery represents a huge sector of retail in most of the countries where online retailing has already achieved significant general penetration. And yet this online penetration doesn't stretch into the grocery sector. Even the in UK, by far the most developed online grocery market in the world, where online retail overall represents over 10% of all retail sales, penetration of online grocery is only around the 4% mark. Theoretically there is a still huge potential for growth worldwide. A closer look at the business model, however, demonstrates why penetration is not greater, and why an apparently untapped opportunity remains to a large extent just that - untapped.

Webvan was perhaps *the* iconic failure of the dotcom bubble. Google for it and you'll find lots of analysis of what went wrong, but they could all be summed up fairly simply: online grocery is very difficult to operate profitably on a cart-by-cart basis, economies of scale are limited, and so pursuing a growth strategy is liable to just grow losses on a cart-by-cart basis with no end in sight. Consider for a moment a typical shopping cart from another online retailer who pursued a growth strategy with more success: Amazon. They don't publish average cart sizes, but let's take a reasonable example of a £25 cart (I'm going to keep the currency in this chapter consistently in GBP, for reasons that will become apparent shortly) with two or three items in it. Gross margin on books is typically 40%. Let's assume the worst possible case – free shipping and no other fee income. The £25 cart is generating £10 of gross profit, out of which all the costs of handling the cart have to be paid. Shipping might be £2.50, packaging materials £0.50, labour costs in picking three items another £0.50, and a whole bunch of miscellaneous additional costs such as payment processing, contacts-per-order, returns handling etc, perhaps contribute another £1.50. That leaves £5 in net profit. In other words, the <u>delivered</u>

margin (see **Chapter 22**) is around 10% (this helps illustrate why delivered margin is such a critical KPI for an online business).

It's possible to repeat the delivered margin exercise for online grocery with some level of confidence, because helpfully there is an online grocery pure-play, Ocado in the UK, which is a publicly quoted company and which publishes sufficient statistics in its annual reports to permit its business model to be approximately reverse engineered with some intelligent guesswork. Ocado is large enough (gross sales in 2011 of £643M) for economies of scale to be well established, but on a delivered margin basis, Ocado essentially operated in 2011, the latest year for which full results are available, at break-even.

Having talked about various online pureplays, what then is this chapter doing in the section of the book on multichannel? The answer lies in taking a look at what changes could be made to the Ocado business model to move it from break-even to profitability. Many of them, and in fact those mainly adopted most retailers who are genuinely able to operate online grocery profitably, rely to a large extent on multichannel. Before investigating these further, let's take a more detailed look at the Ocado model.

28.2   Case Study Details

Before heading into the analysis, I'd just like to get the caveats out on the table. Ocado publishes a lot of data[119], but there is still a great deal it does not publish. A big dollop of approximation and guesstimation is still required in order to derive meaningful conclusions. Although I've shown figures to the nearest penny in order to make up the picture and get totals to add up to 100%, they should certainly not be regarded as accurate to the nearest penny. There is also a risk that details of the calculations are simply wrong, and/or that some key factor is omitted. However, having tested this cart-by-cart approach to online food on some client assignments, I believe the

---

[119]   See   http://www.ocadogroup.com/investor-centre/results-and-presentations/pr-2011.aspx. All quotes in this section are taken from the 2011 annual report

broad conclusions are still valid, and I'd request that you look at the top-level picture without getting too bogged down in the precision of the calculations. I've supplied details of the calculations to assist anyone who wants to build their own model, and because some of the reasoning helps illustrate key points about online grocery as a proposition.

28.2.1 Delivery fees

Ocado tells us they delivered an average of 110,000 orders per week, equating to 5.73 million over the full year 2001. The first piece of missing information, and therefore the first approximation, is the delivery fee income. Differentiation in online grocery is primarily about convenience, and Ocado rises to this challenge by offering very precise delivery slots; as a customer you can be sure when to wait in for your groceries. These slots – a customer-selected one hour window booked up to 3 weeks ahead – are variably priced like airline tickets: a popular slot is more expensive.

When I first made this analysis, just after the annual results were published in March 2011, I estimated that the average delivery slot charged a fee of £4.75. As I write this sentence on New Year's Day 2013, I've just logged into their website and I can now see that the average delivery slot fee is about £1, with many slots free-of-charge. Like many other online pureplays (see section *18.2*), Ocado is seeing the attractions of offering free delivery. We'll see what impact this might have on the challenging online grocery model in the conclusions. For the purposes of this analysis, I'll stick with the £4.75 estimate that was roughly valid in 2011.

28.2.2 Margin

Although Ocado publishes gross margins of 30%, these include delivery-fee income. Once this is stripped out using the above estimate, gross margins are around 26%. By food retail standards this is still a pretty respectable number.

It's worth briefly considering whether higher margins might be achievable online than in store. Online grocery shoppers are primarily motivated by convenience first, price second. The stereotypical persona is a middle-class working mother with two or more young children - cash-rich, time-poor — who will buy at least some premium products. Online grocery carts also typically include a larger percentage of the sort of bulky items on which margins may be higher.

28.2.3 Overview of average cart sales and margin

Bringing the previous two calculations together into an overview of the income half of the story, we find the picture shown in **Figure 92**, for an average order cart after sales taxes.

Figure 92 - Ocado cart, income breakdown

28.2.4 Costs introduction

Now for the costs side of the same average cart. We'll use the definition provided by Ocado themselves:

"Distribution costs consist of all the cost incurred, excluding product costs, to the point of sale, usually the customer's home. This includes the payroll-related expenses for the picking, dispatch and delivery of the product sold to the point of sale, the cost of making those

deliveries, including fuel, tolls, maintenance of vehicles, the operating costs of the properties required for the picking, dispatch and onward delivery operations and all associated depreciation, amortisation and impairment charges, call-centre costs and payment processing charges."

Ocado tell us that altogether this cost them £151M in FY2011. How does this break-down?

28.2.5 Last mile delivery

A major complication for an online grocer attempting to offer customers a complete online weekly-grocery-shop is the multiple product storage requirements. Fresh, chilled, frozen, bakery, super-fresh (seafood for example), room-temperature products are all involved. Ocado, in common with other such home-delivery services, uses specialist delivery vans equipped for these multiple product types.

A very useful statistic they publish is the number of deliveries made by each such van: 145 per week. Their deliveries operate from 6:30am to 11:30pm seven days a week. Making a few allowances for operating processes, we can estimate that an average delivery requires around 49 minutes, including both travel time and handover time on the doorstep.

A lot more approximation is required to turn this into financials, including factors such as the hourly cost of drivers, likely distance between drops (a figure that unfortunately is not published) based on average road speeds, fuel prices, and the likely cost of specialised vans. My estimations are that the costs per order for Ocado are £1.81 for fuel, £1.31 for other vehicle costs, and £6.57 for drivers' time. Deriving these figures requires long chains of assumption and estimation. Anyone making a model for online grocery themselves, rather than reverse engineering somebody else's, will be able to make much more accurate models. The critical factor in countries with high labour costs is the time between deliveries, and in countries with lower labour costs it is the distance and consequent fuel consumption and vehicle wear-and-tear. More generally, drop-density is the key KPI. All successful online grocery propositions for home-delivery concentrate first on densely populated urban areas (that also contain enough cash-rich time-poor consumers). Any rollout strategy should be planned on a district by district basis.

Before the assumptions get too risky to be credible, fortunately Ocado also publishes a statistic for the total cost of deliveries:

"Trunking and delivery costs fell as a percentage of revenue from 13.2% in 2010 to 12.9% in 2011"

If the above estimates are accurate, then the remaining - trunking - equates to £3.76 per order. Even if all these assumptions mean the previous individual data points are somewhat off the mark, this published benchmark provides an overall sanity check.

28.2.6 Warehousing and picking

Ocado helpfully tell us the overall operating cost of their central warehouse: 11.3% of revenues. They operate a large, highly automated, single central warehouse (they are currently building a second one), and then if necessary trunk the picked orders to spoke depots from which the specialised vans make the last-mile deliveries.

Even more helpfully, they provide a labour efficiency measure for this central warehouse: 111 units picked per hour per man-hour of labour. And they tell us how many items are in each order:

"...picking an average of over 50 items per order from over 20,000 SKUs across three temperature zones with different product life (ambient, chilled and frozen)."

So roughly it still takes <u>half-a-man-hour to pick a grocery order</u>, even in a highly sophisticated and automated warehouse. With some reasonable assumptions for the hourly costs of labour, again it's possible to estimate the costs-per-order at £3.80 per order, and the remaining costs of the central warehouse at £8.04 per order.

28.2.7 Other costs

Other costs per order are relatively insignificant. Online grocery generates less contacts-per-order than most other models, partly because items are very standard, but mainly because queries are typically resolved on the doorstep. I estimate around £0.38 per order.

Fraud is a relatively insignificant in online food, and so payment processing costs are generally low. I estimate around £0.83 per order.

28.2.8 Overview of average cart costs

Bringing all these calculations (and assumptions!) together, we end up with the picture in *Figure 93*.

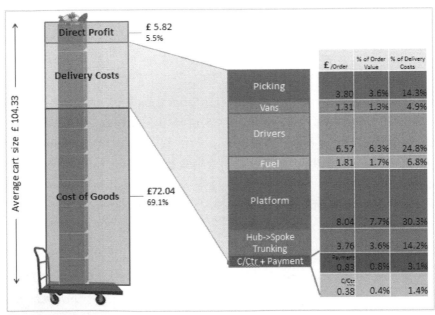

Figure 93 - Ocado cart, cost breakdown

28.3   Case Study Summary

28.3.1 Online pure-play perspective

The challenge of online grocery profitability is most clearly illustrated when we set Ocado's costs and income per average cart side by side (*Figure 94).*

Figure 94 - Ocado, costs and income per average cart

Direct Profit of 5.5% is measured before non-cart related expenses (head-office costs) are taken into account. Once these are added to the mix then an average cart with a tax-inclusive cost to the customer of £112.15 generates a net profit of £0.18, equivalent to 0.16%. The potential impact of following non-food online pure-plays by reducing delivery fee income is stark.

A critical limitation in the business model is that carts smaller than £82.50 are actually unprofitable. Suddenly the size of the potential market decreases violently – how many grocery shopping carts are larger than this number? If we estimate that only 25% of grocery sales by value are in carts larger than this threshold, then the penetration of online into overall UK grocery restricted to above-threshold carts changes from 4% to 16%, which is magically just about consistent with non-food penetration.

Ocado's approach to improving the situation includes increasing cart-size by increasing their assortment, reducing trunking costs by adding another central warehouse in another part of the country, and continuing to drive the efficiency of their platform and picking. Ideally they'd also like to drive up that crucial KPI last-mile drop density, but against stiff local competition that isn't so easy to do. As an online pure-play, their options are somewhat limited.

28.3.2 Multichannel perspective

Now take a look from a multichannel point of view. A lot more of those unpleasant costs can be attacked in some way. One option is to get rid of all those difficult last-mile delivery costs (although also the delivery fee), by simply not offering last-mile delivery. Customers like click-and-collect, and in fact in food it potentially allows the customer to blend their order by picking those difficult fresh items themselves, rather than writing hopeful – and time-consuming for the retailer - notes to the picker. (An anecdotal story, which I can't resist repeating here: a customer who specified that a turnip should have a skin with a pattern like a smiley face. Her home delivery duly arrived with a turnip just as specified, with a handwritten annotation from the picker "glad to be of service.") Current examples of click-and-collect grocery include Colruyt (Belgium), Carrefour (France), Real (Germany) and Tesco are now rolling it out in the UK alongside their home-delivery service[120].

Picking from store is an obvious corollary. As with most truly multichannel retailing, this requires some changes to existing operating models. Picking-efficiency is still an essential element of the profitability of the model, and so the replenishment of stock onto shelves now has to become a tightly controlled process where every item goes into a (semi-)predictable location; this both increases

---

[120] Where it already represents 5% of Tesco's online grocery business; see Christmas and New Year Trading Statement, January 2013

complexity and in-store labour costs. There is a risk of KPI-driven pickers stampeding real customers, so timing has to be managed carefully.

Store picking has another advantage. An online grocery fulfilment centre is a specialised affair, with its multiple temperature zones and difficult to pick-for-customer items (think loose tomatoes or fresh fish). Non-food fulfilment is fairly standard, and so it is relatively easy to scale warehousing space to match the volume of business. Not so for food if you follow the Ocado central-warehouse model; a new specialised fulfilment centre is a major step-change. Store picking, by contrast, is relatively easy to scale. Platform costs are not zero – modifications are required to the store for marshalling and loading orders – but they are modest on a store-by-store basis. If you are offering a home-delivery service, store-picking also acts as an automatic incentive to drive the critical drop-density KPI by localising it.

28.4   Other differences from non-food

There are various other differences between online grocery and non-food which mean that "standard" online solutions, especially IT packages, are challenging to apply. In no particular order these issues include:

Large carts: a typical non-food shopping cart will have two or three items in it, and will rarely have more than a dozen. A typical food shopping cart, at the sort of minimum size necessary for profitability, will have over fifty items. Many standard software packages, and also user interfaces, will find this stressful to handle.

Substitutions: if a customer orders a Sony camera, you are out of stock, and so you instead supply a Canon camera of a similar specification, your customer is unlikely to be very impressed. The opposite applies to food. If you are out of stock of the 500g pack of butter, 2 x 250g packs or an alternative brand will almost certainly be accepted instead, and in fact the customer would rather experience this situation than be out of butter. Picking processes, and other related operating processes, need to take this into account. Substitutions represent a time consuming and costly part of picking, and yet a 50 item cart requires better than 98.6% stock availability to be picked at less than an even chance of at least one substitution, a very challenging target indeed. Many online grocery sites also have specific interface areas for the customer to indicate what policy they would like applying in the event of an out-of-stock.

Loose-weight and catch-weight products: many customers prefer to add apples to cart by the apple, not by the kilogramme, even though they may still be priced by weight. Meat or fish is almost always priced by kilogramme, even though the customer may simply want a whole joint or whole fish. Alternatively if the customer does prefer to buy by the kilogramme, they typically want a fraction – 0.2Kg for example. The user-interface, and supporting software, needs to be capable of operating in alternative or fractional units.

Price-after-pick: because of substitutions and weight-based products, an online grocery order typically cannot be finally priced until picking is complete. The following two quotes show an example policy, and are especially interesting because the proposition is actually B2B not B2C – Booker, whose website these are taken from[121], is a food wholesaler with a £500M+ store-picked online food delivery business:

"The guide prices shown online are the prices that are currently valid in-store, albeit these prices are only a guide as to what your total order may cost at the time of processing. Prices charged will be the cost of products you have ordered at the time of picking and

---

[121] www.booker.co.uk

processing your order, and as a result they may be different to the price shown on the website at the time of order."

"All of our promotions and special offers are displayed on the website as soon as they become available. Please note however that the invoice price will be applied at the time of picking and processing your order, and not at the point of ordering. You should therefore ensure that you check any validity periods of promotions and offers..."

Delivery scheduling: offering, as Ocado does, specific one-hour delivery slots three weeks ahead with dynamic pricing by slot-capacity requires some sophisticated – and therefore expensive – scheduling software and systems.

Favourites: the first time you try and online grocery shopping site can be enough to put you off for ever. As a simple illustration of why, please think of a canned product that you routinely keep in your store-cupboard (and not beer!). Now, without going and looking at it, tell me if you usually buy the 141g/5oz can, the 198g/7oz can, or the 255g/9oz can. Oh yes, and how many mangoes make up 1.6Kg/3lb? The equivalent on Amazon would be if I asked you to purchase your 60 favourite books of all time, but I insisted on specifying exactly which edition you had to choose. An average unaided first-time user of a grocery site will take over 45 minutes to place an order for a weekly shop. Having completed this awful task once, given that the proposition is supposed to be all about convenience, a customer will expect it to be easier next time around. The sites therefore remember what each customer has bought recently – their favourites - and offer a tick-cross shopping list facility. A nice multichannel extension of this is listing favourites from loyalty card data gathered offline, in order to help overcome the first-time shop barrier. Once again, this is specialist functionality which is largely irrelevant to non-food categories.

28.5 Alternative models

Given the foregoing, it's perhaps less than surprising that multichannel penetration of the grocery sector lags behind other categories globally. The full weekly-groceries-shop model is both complex and very far removed from "standard" models of online retail. Some alternative food models, therefore, seek to avoid the majority of the complexity and/or operate in a more nearly standard way.

A large proportion of the complexity is caused by the need for mixed temperature zones, and consequent specialist warehousing, picking and delivery vehicles. Amazon itself has a beta in Germany and the UK of a food offer which excludes all those awkward things - only long-life products that can be added to cart as a single unit are available. The result is a fairly bizarre assortment, and serves as a nice illustration of the difficulty of trying to fit food into non-food systems and processes.

A more plausible alternative is adopted by online stores offering organic or local produce, such as Aussie Farmers Direct in Australia or Riverford in the UK. Warehousing and picking costs are minimised by offering only a very limited assortment, often "fixed" weekly box-sets – one item for order management purposes, although containing many different pieces. Difficult temperature zones like frozen are excluded. In general the proposition is that you get high quality fresh staples from the online offer, but still go elsewhere – less frequently – for your other needs. Distribution costs are reduced by franchising, which has the side-benefit of incentivising drop-density. Long duration doorstep handovers are minimised by few items-per-cart and by generally avoiding specific substitutions.

28.6 Top Takeaways

Online grocery is a potentially very large opportunity. Penetration of online into food is very limited in most countries. However it has a challenging operating model. Analysis of online grocery models should proceed on a cart-by-cart basis.

A case-study, Ocado, illustrates a finely balanced business model. The costs of highly convenient last mile delivery combined with multi-zone (fresh, super-fresh, frozen, chilled, bakery, room-temperature) product management and fulfilment can soon eat up gross margins. Drop density is an extremely critical KPI.

High order lifecycle costs demand very large average cart-sizes to reach break-even; this limits the size of the potential market.

Other features of online grocery models which are different to non-food models include very large numbers of items in carts, substitutions, loose- and catch-weight products, price-after-pick, favourites, and complex delivery scheduling.

A multichannel approach can eliminate or reduce some of the cost burden, making it profitable. Collect-in-store offers already exist in many countries, eliminating delivery costs. Pick-in-store operations can significantly reduce order handing costs.

Alternative models can also be successful, such as regular boxes of fresh and/or organic produce; they reduce costs by simplifying delivery and not handling a complete range.

Using non-food solutions for an online grocery proposition results in a weird assortment, even for Amazon!

Glossary of Terms

Every discipline has its specialist terms, not necessarily purely in order to confound the outsider. I have tried to avoid jargon other than that which I have defined in the text, but some is inevitable, especially standard "business" jargon such as B2C. Moreover some terms which I have defined in the next nevertheless crop up sufficiently frequently to make it difficult to read an individual chapter standalone if you missed the definition in another chapter, hence the glossary.

A/B testing	The process of simultaneously serving two different experiences to a random cross-section of online customers, and measuring the difference in the results. See also *analytics*. See **Chapter 21**.
Adaptive Design	Adaptive design (suggested definition): adapting the user experience to fit the capabilities of the device. For example does it support GPS, or pinch-gestures? See **Chapter 25.**
Affiliate	A website which specialises in directing traffic to retailer sites in exchange for a commission on consequently checked out orders. See **Chapter 18**.
Analytics	An aggregated statistical view of the page to page journeys taken by online customers, used to measure the effectiveness of website customer experience in delivering goals. See **Chapter 21**.
ATP	Available to Promise. A description of the stock promise to online customers. See **Chapter 16.**
B2B	Business to Business
B2C	Business to Consumer
BIN Range	The first 6 digits of a credit card number,

which define the issuing scheme and country of the issuer.

Bricks'n'clicks'n'flicks   The mixture of online, brick-and-mortar and paper (e.g. catalogue) retailing.

Broadband   Has different exact meanings in different countries. Generally used to refer to fixed-line connectivity which is faster than 56K dial-up modem, or to mobile connectivity provided by 3G or 4G networks.

C2C   Consumer to Consumer – typically used to describe marketplaces such as eBay or TaoBao.

Cannibalisation   One sales channel taking sales away from another; typically used to refer to the switch of sales from brick-and-mortar to online channels within a single retailer.

Channel conflict   Describes a retailer whose sales channels compete not collaborate with each other, most commonly competition between online and brick-and-mortar. See *Chapter 12.*

Click-and-collect   An order online, collect from store proposition. See Chapter 26.

Click-through-rate   The percentage of clicks to displays of an element on a screen.

CNP   Card Not Present or Customer Not Present. Usually in the context of credit/debit cards payments via websites.

Conversion rate   The percentage of visits to a store which result in a checkout.

CRM   Customer Relationship Management

Cross-channel   The joining up of retail channels from checkout and afterwards. See *Chapter 9.*

D2C   Direct to Consumer – used to describe manufacturers or brands selling direct to end consumers, bypassing the retailer.

DC
Distribution Centre. Warehouse used to replenish brick-and-mortar stores. Used as a term to distinguish from an online order Fulfilment Centre.

Delivered Margin
Margin including delivery fee income but minus shipping costs (and other order lifecycle costs). See *Chapter 22*.

DSV
Drop Ship Vendor – a supplier which accepts orders from retailer websites and sends the goods directly to the end-customer. See *Chapter 20.*

Endless aisle
A category assortment containing a much broader range of products than can fit into a brick-and-mortar store aisle, because it includes a long tail.

ERP
Enterprise Resource Management (System)

FC
Fulfilment Centre. Warehouse used to process customer orders. Used as a term to distinguish from Distribution Centre.

FTE
Full Time Equivalent – one employee working full time.

Kompetenz
A word borrowed from German to describe a good multichannel assortment, having capability, authority, competence, jurisdiction. See *Chapter 6*

KPI
Key Performance Indicator.

Long tail
Products which complete a range but are by no means the best-sellers which might fit into a store.

Merchandising
Used in a narrower sense to describe *how* products are sold; includes various practices such as cross-selling, up-selling, personalisation, recommendations

Omni-channel	The joining up of the customer's experience up to and including checkout. See *Chapter 9.*
OMS	Order Management Systems
One Second Rule	See *0.* A way to describe the rapidity of customers to assess if an online screen is worth further attention
Order Lifecycle	Everything that happens to an order from checkout onwards. See *Chapter 20*.
P.R.I.C.E.	Differentiation framework based around 5 factors: Price, Range, Information, Convenience, Experience. See *Chapter 4* and following.
Payment Gateway	A service for processing customer payments online. See Chapter 20.
Payment policy	When money for an online order is taken from the customer. Typically one of on-despatch, on-order, on-delivery. See *Chapter 20.*
Personalisation	Varying a proposition for each customer to offer an individual customer the things like are most likely to buy
Price Transparency	An effect of online retailing in a market or country: prices for all standard products are available for customers to research and compare
PSP	Payment Service Provider – see payment gateway
Pure-play	A retailer which sells only online, with no brick-and-mortar stores.
Range	Synonym for assortment.
Responsive Design	Ensuring each page caters for the layout of any device that might be accessing it, by changing itself to fit. See *Chapter 25.*
Searchandising	Solutions which blend merchandising and

search.

SEM	Search Engine Marketing
SEO	Search Engine Optimisation
Showrooming	The customer practice of visiting brick-and-mortar stores purely to touch and feel products which they subsequently buy online.
Silver Surfer	An older internet user, characterised by a mixture of careful research and higher spending power.
SKU	Stock keeping unit. Usually a synonym for product.
TaoBao	China's answer to eBay.
UCD	User Centric Design
WMS	Warehouse Management System

Index

4141947R00163

Printed in Great Britain
by Amazon.co.uk, Ltd.,
Marston Gate.